Scenes from New Aztlán

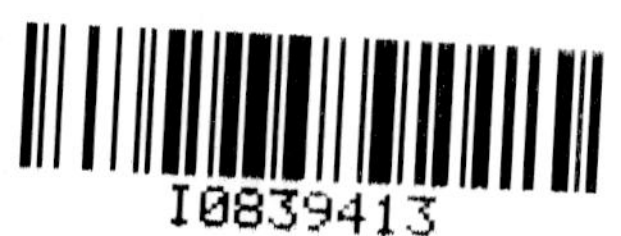

A Coloring Book for Adults

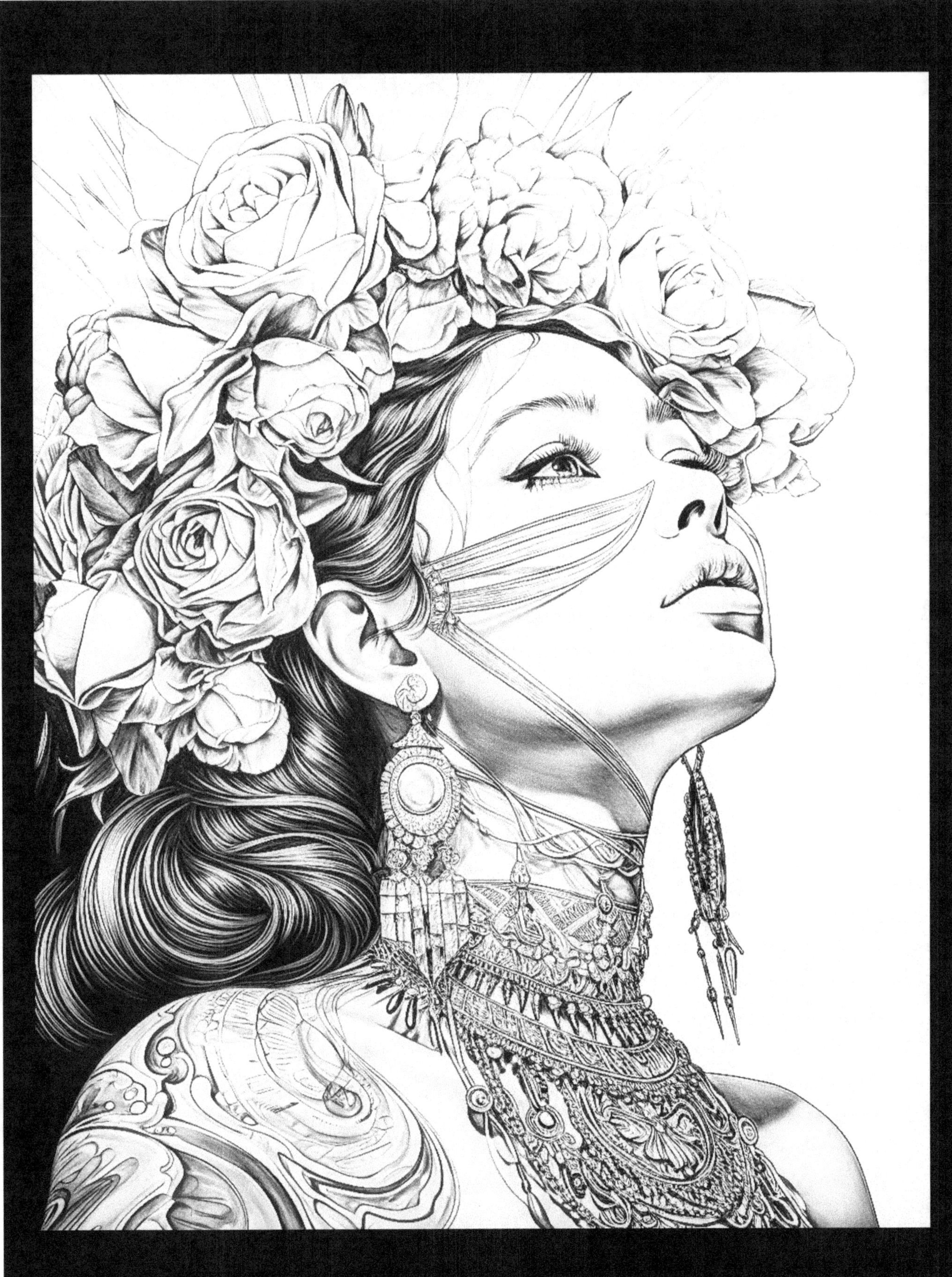

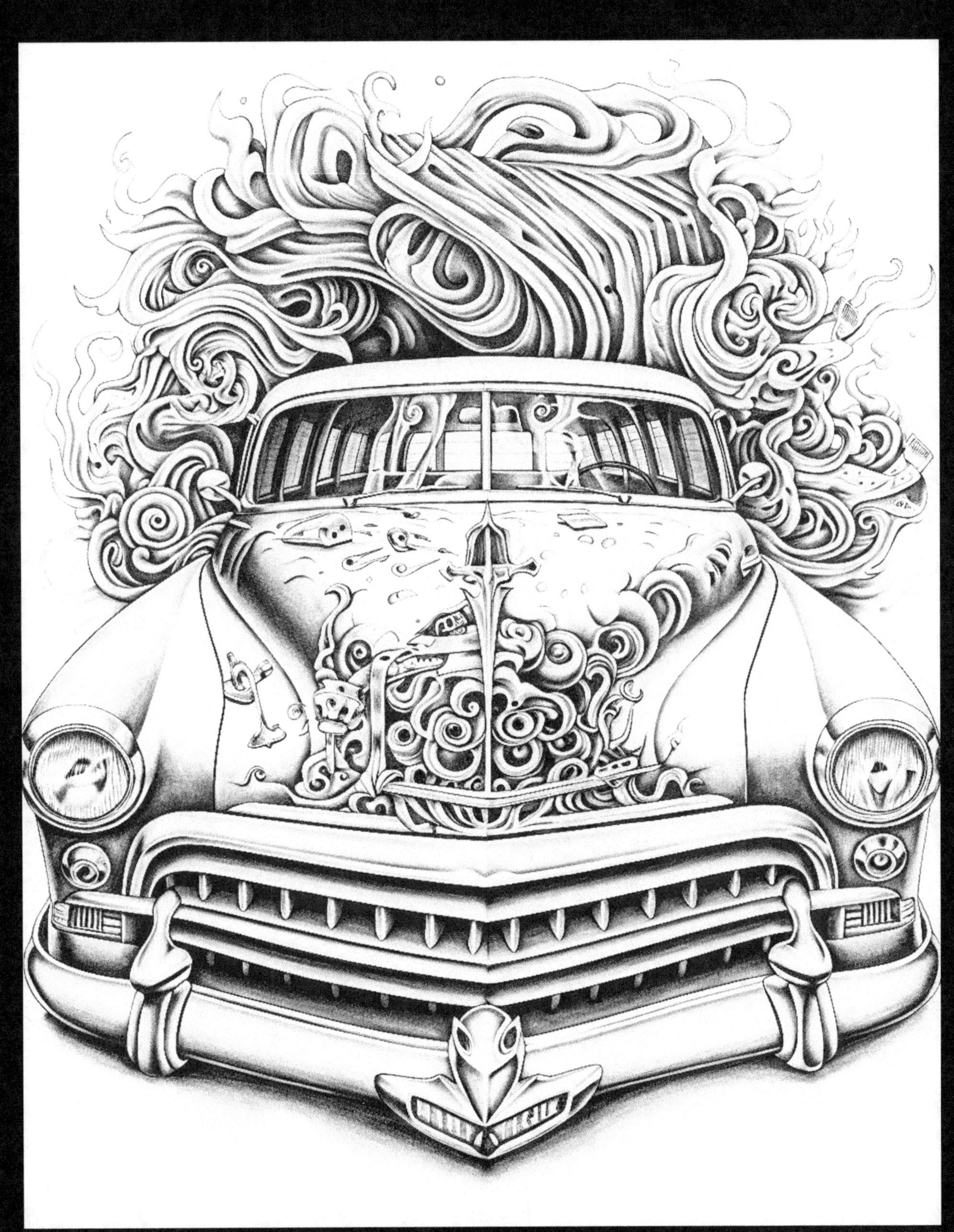

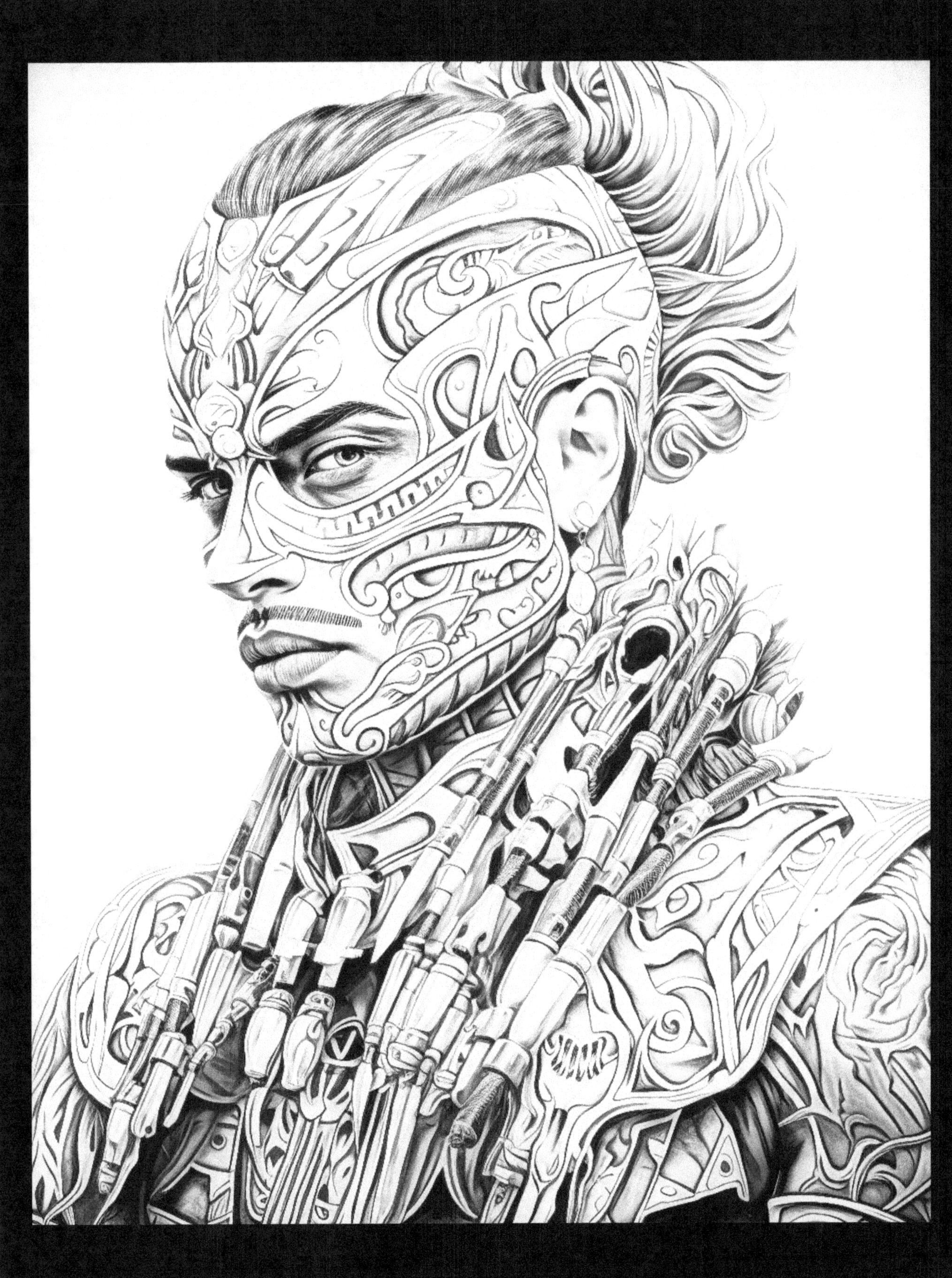

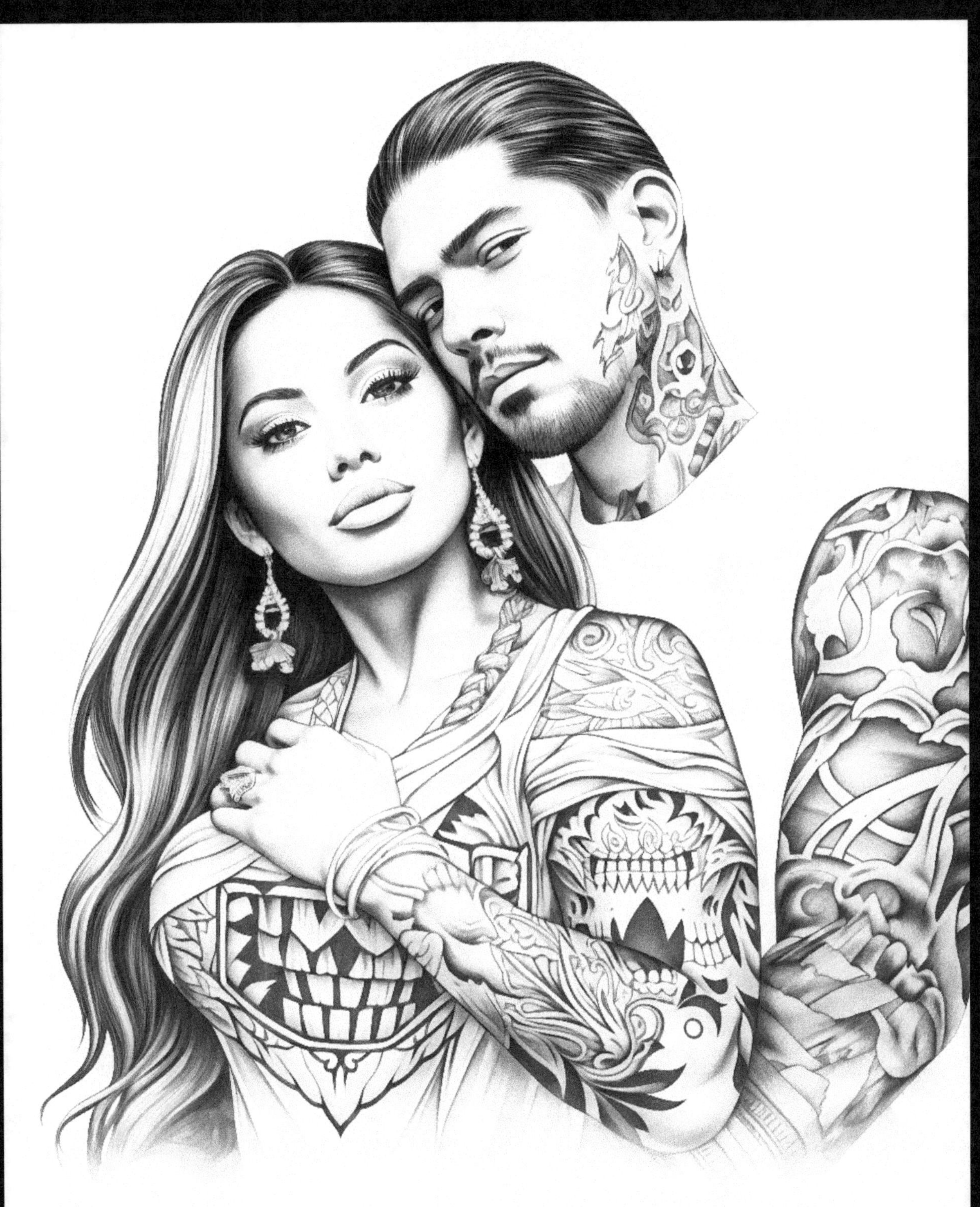

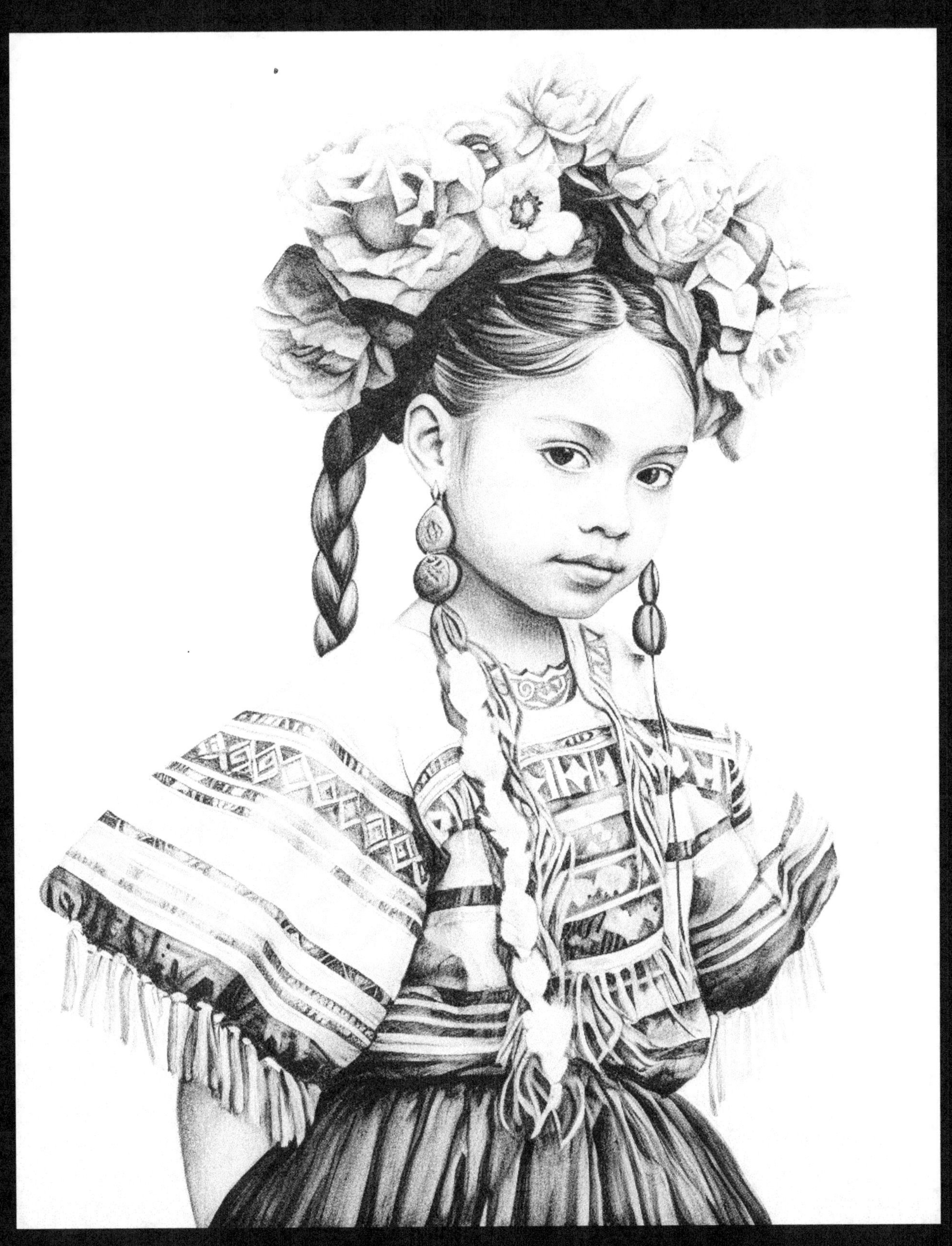

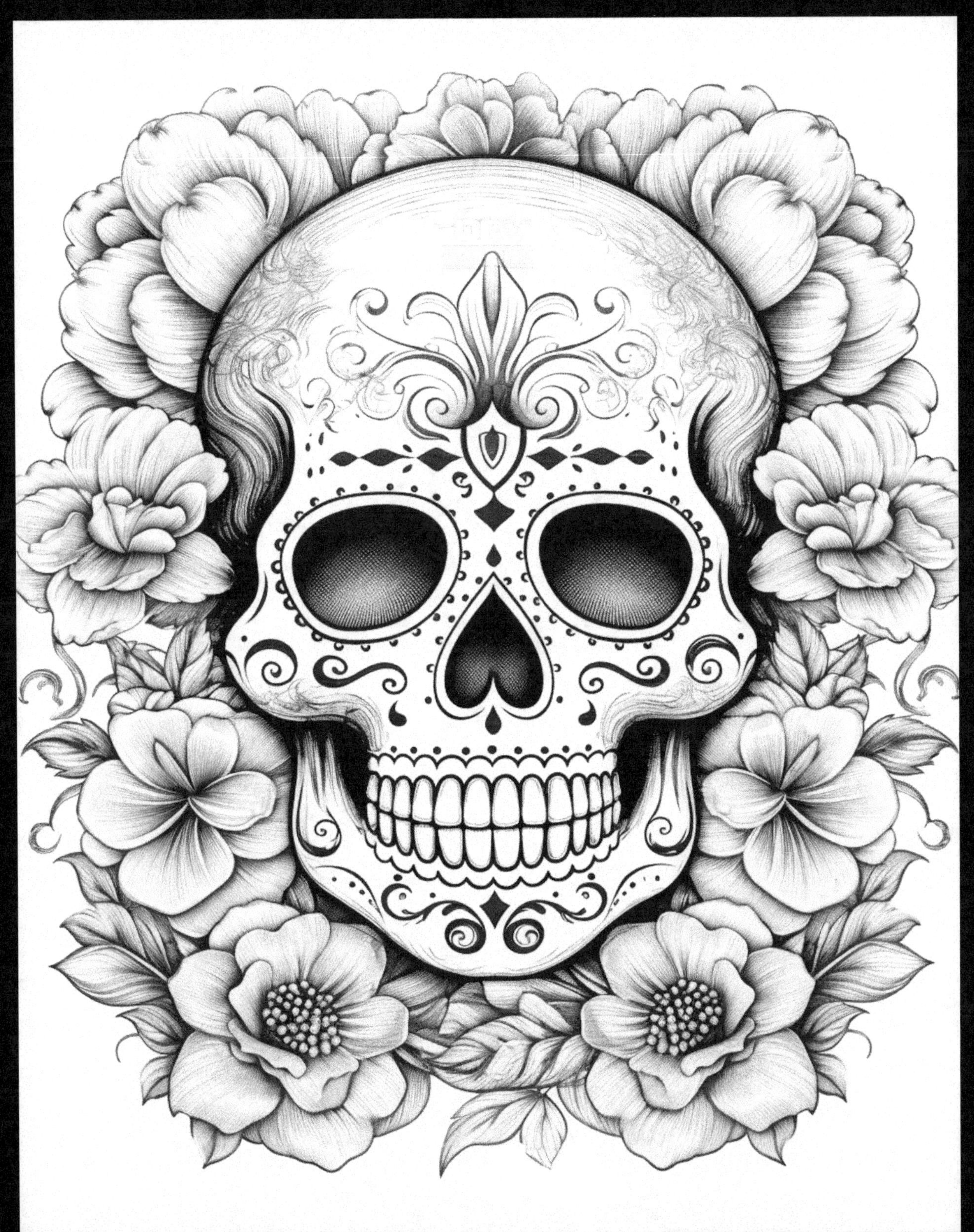

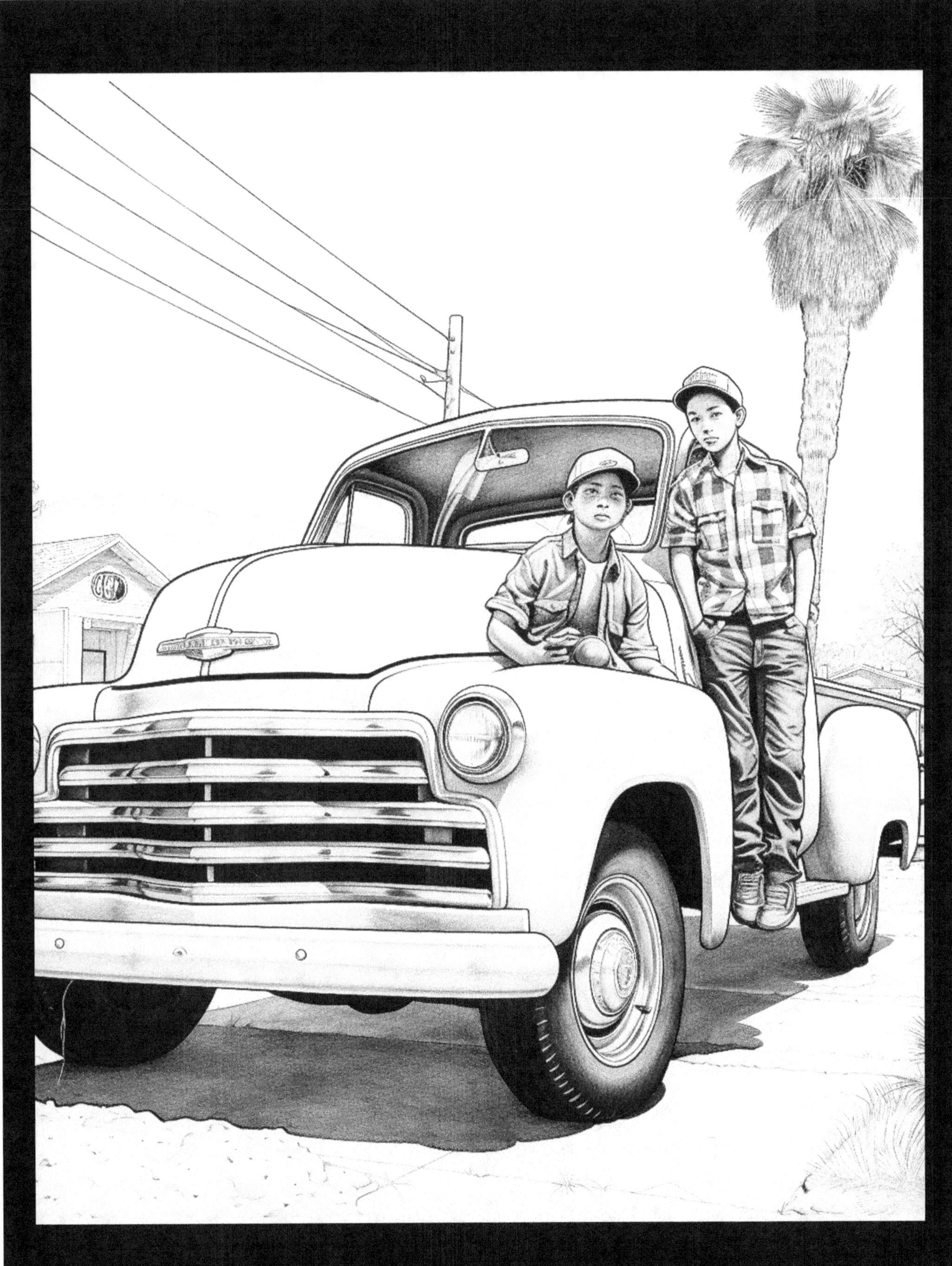

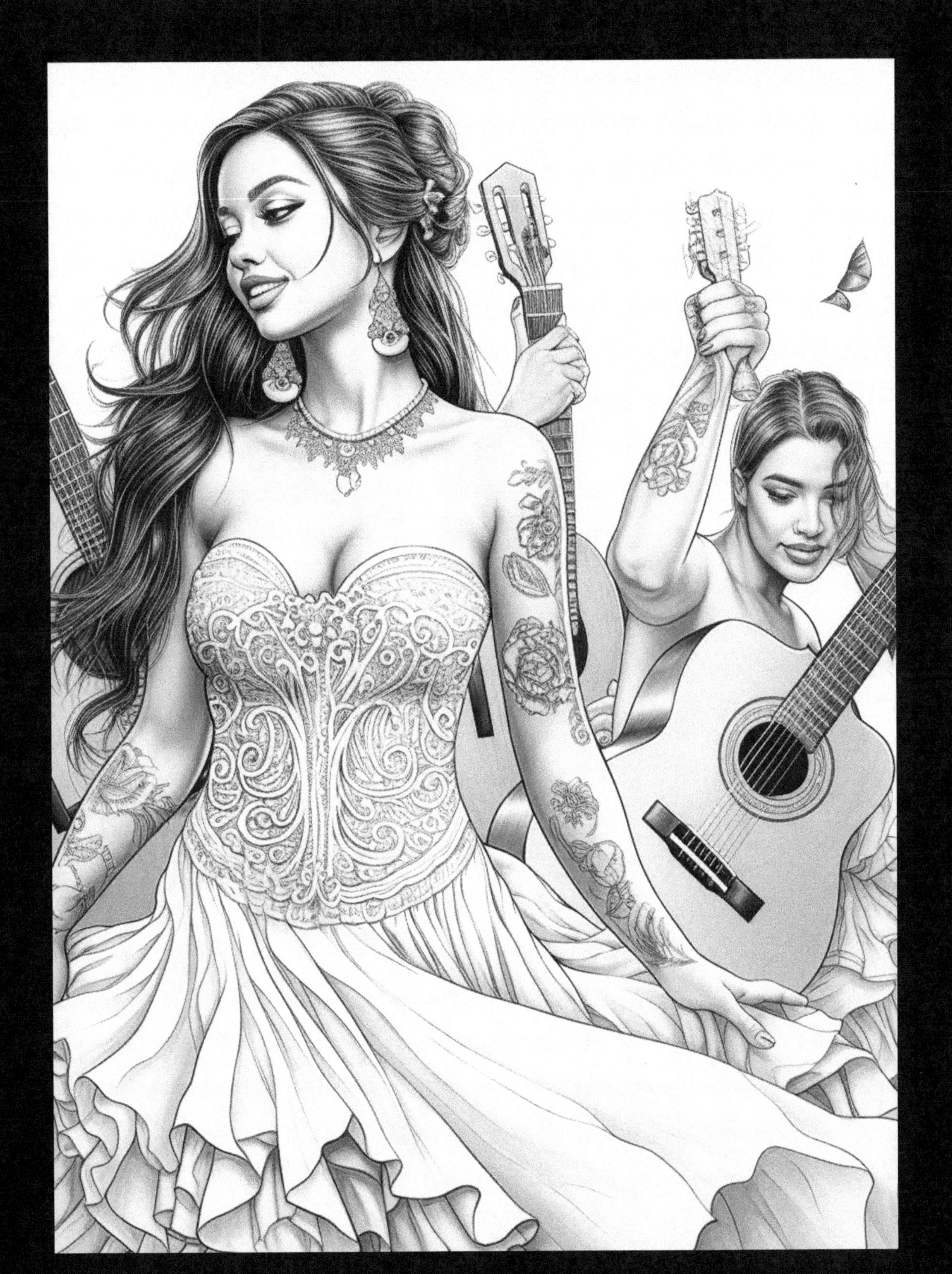

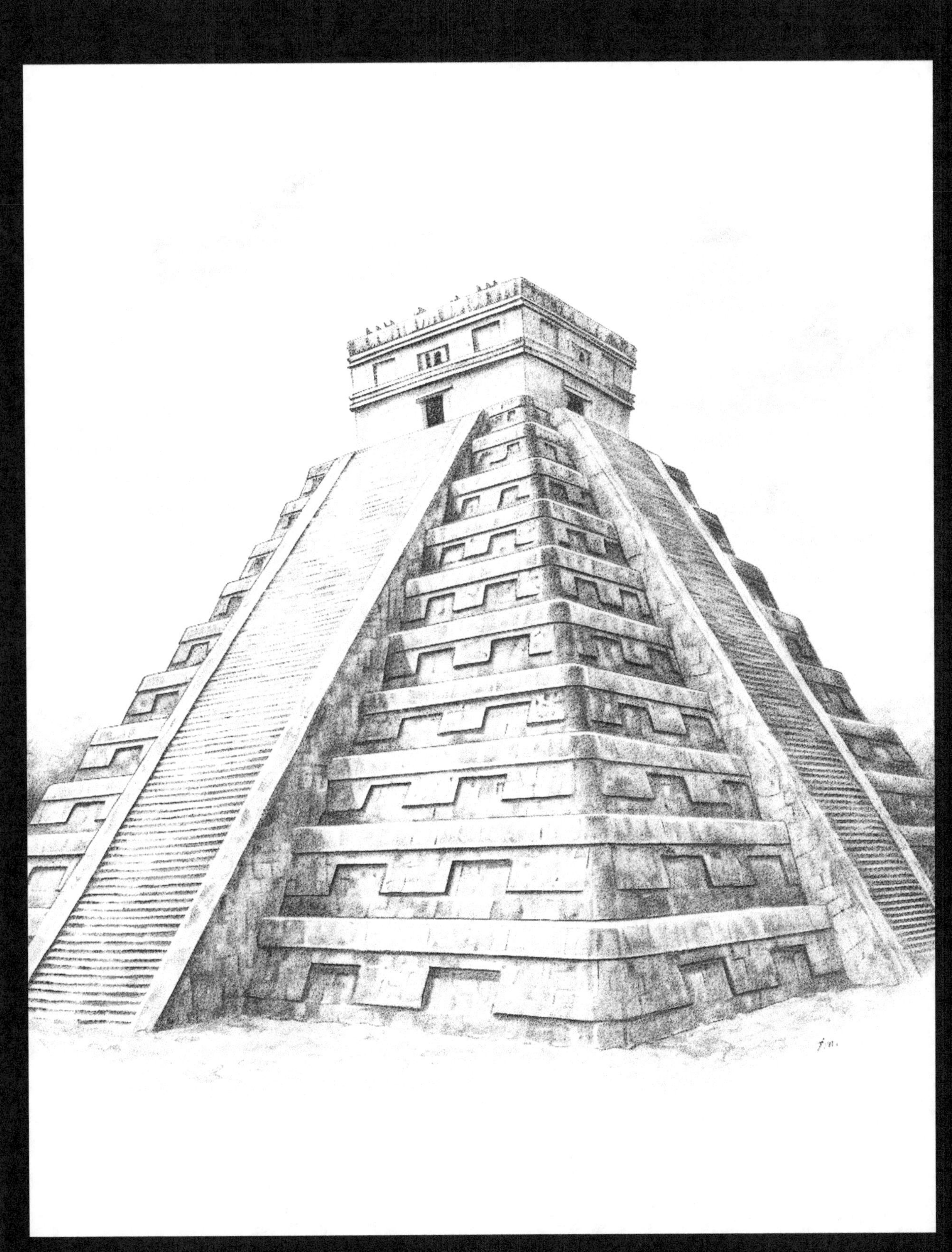

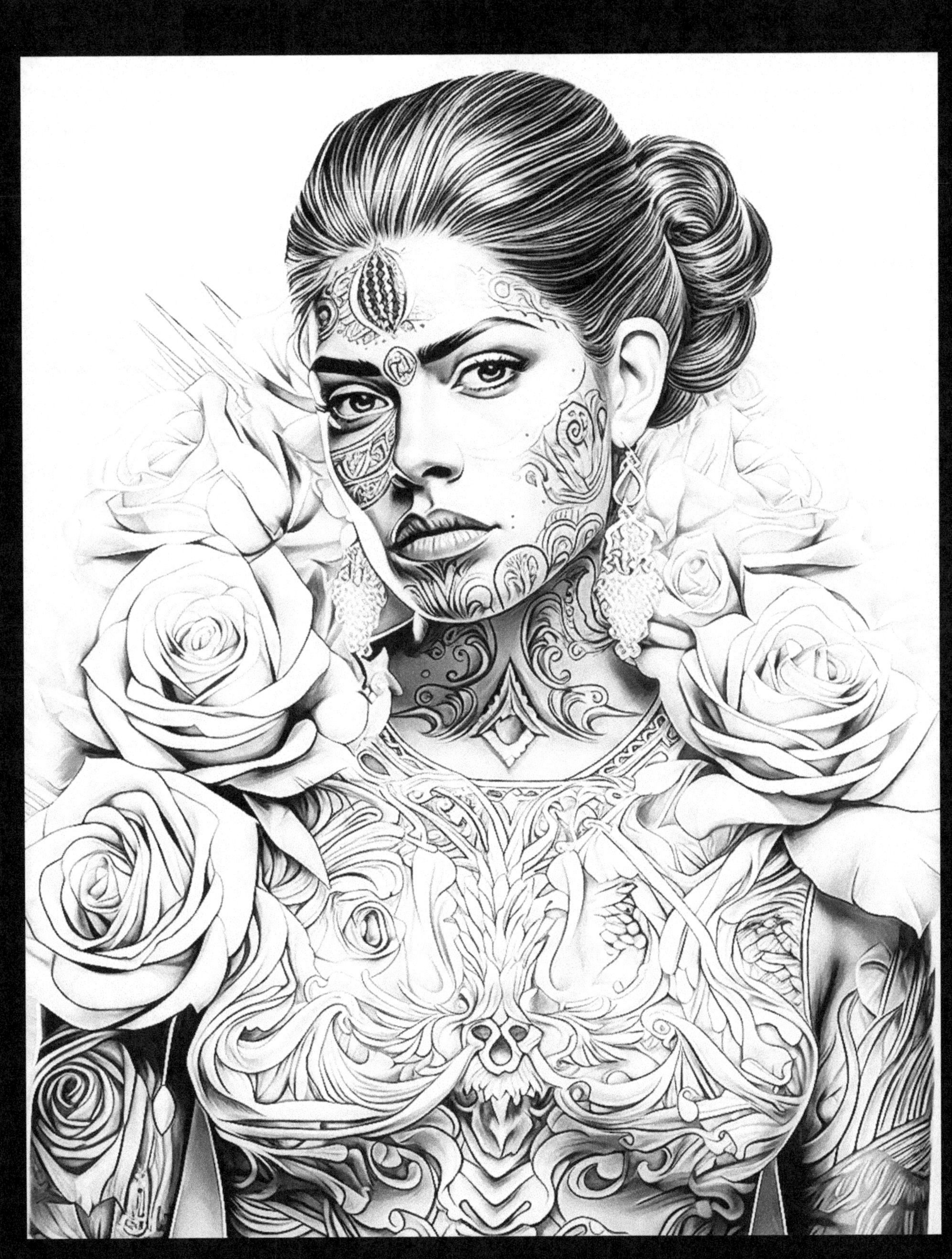

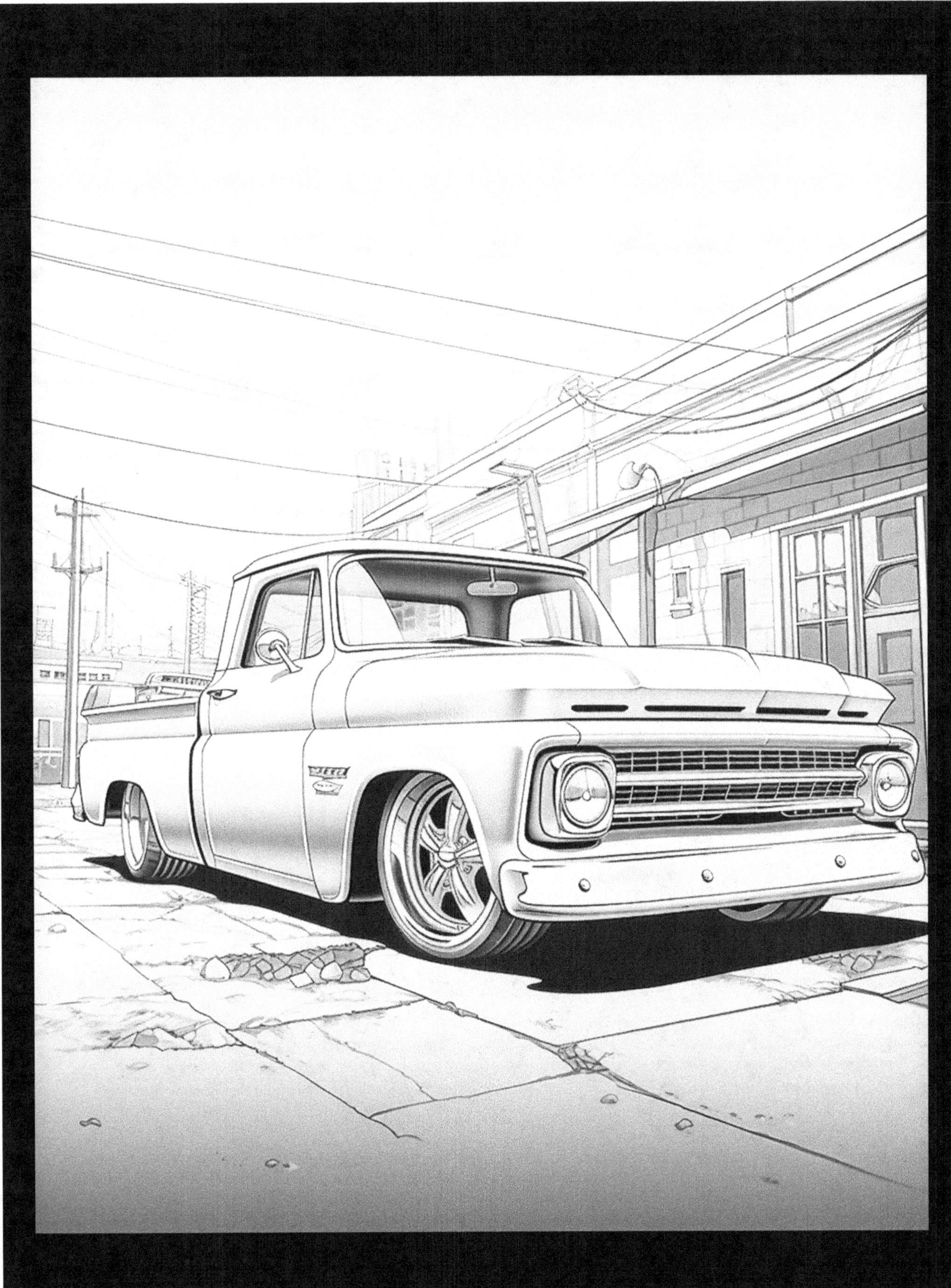

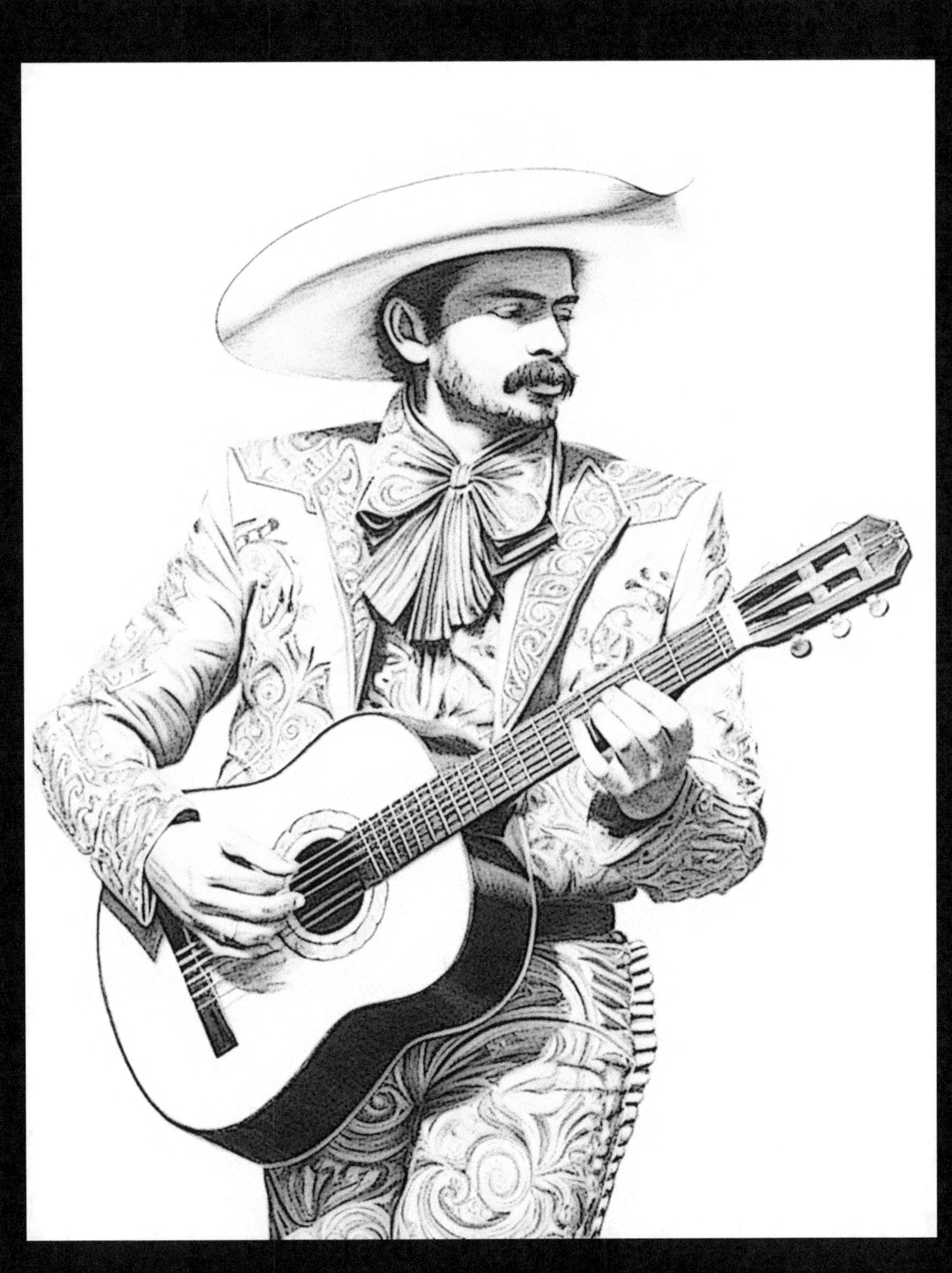

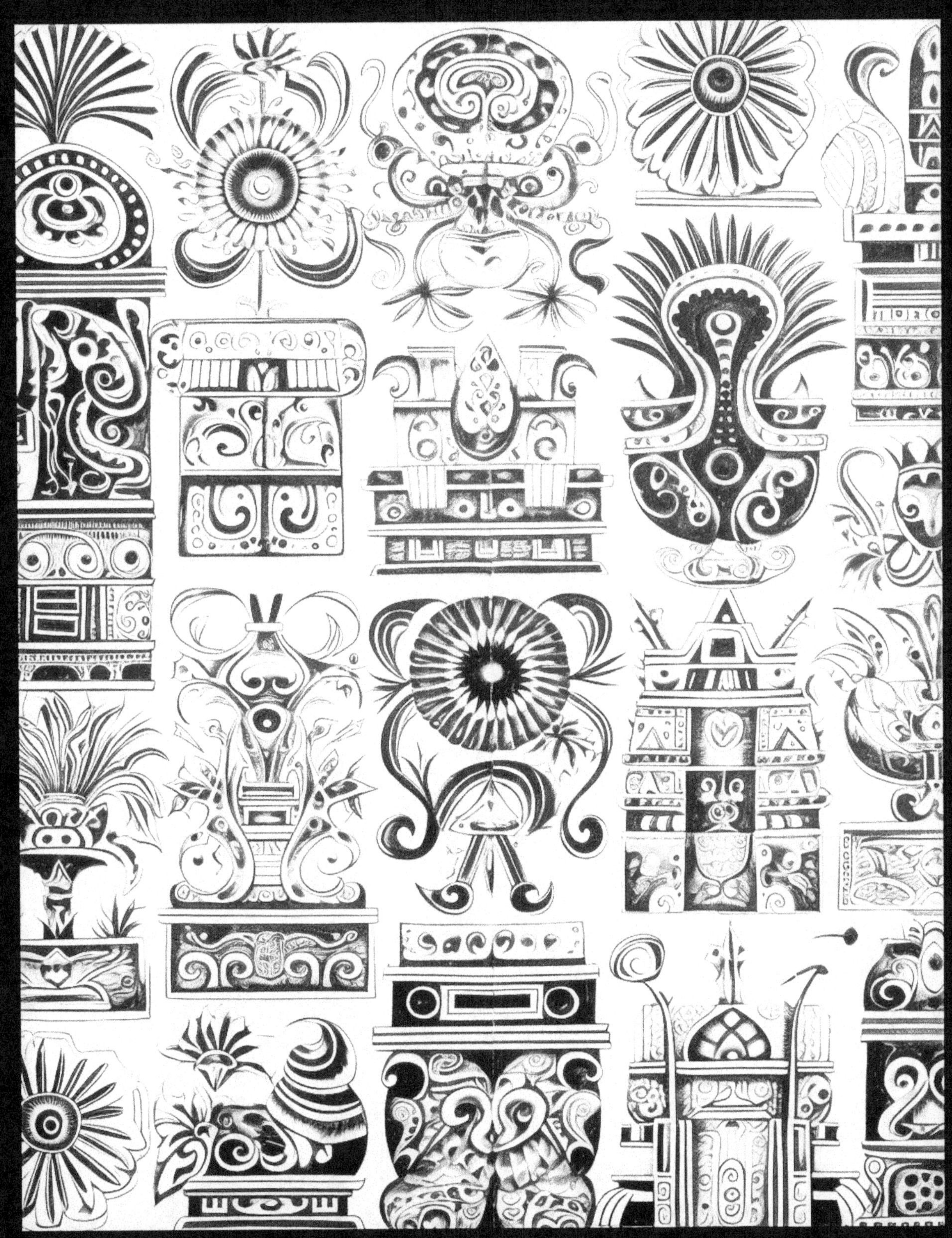

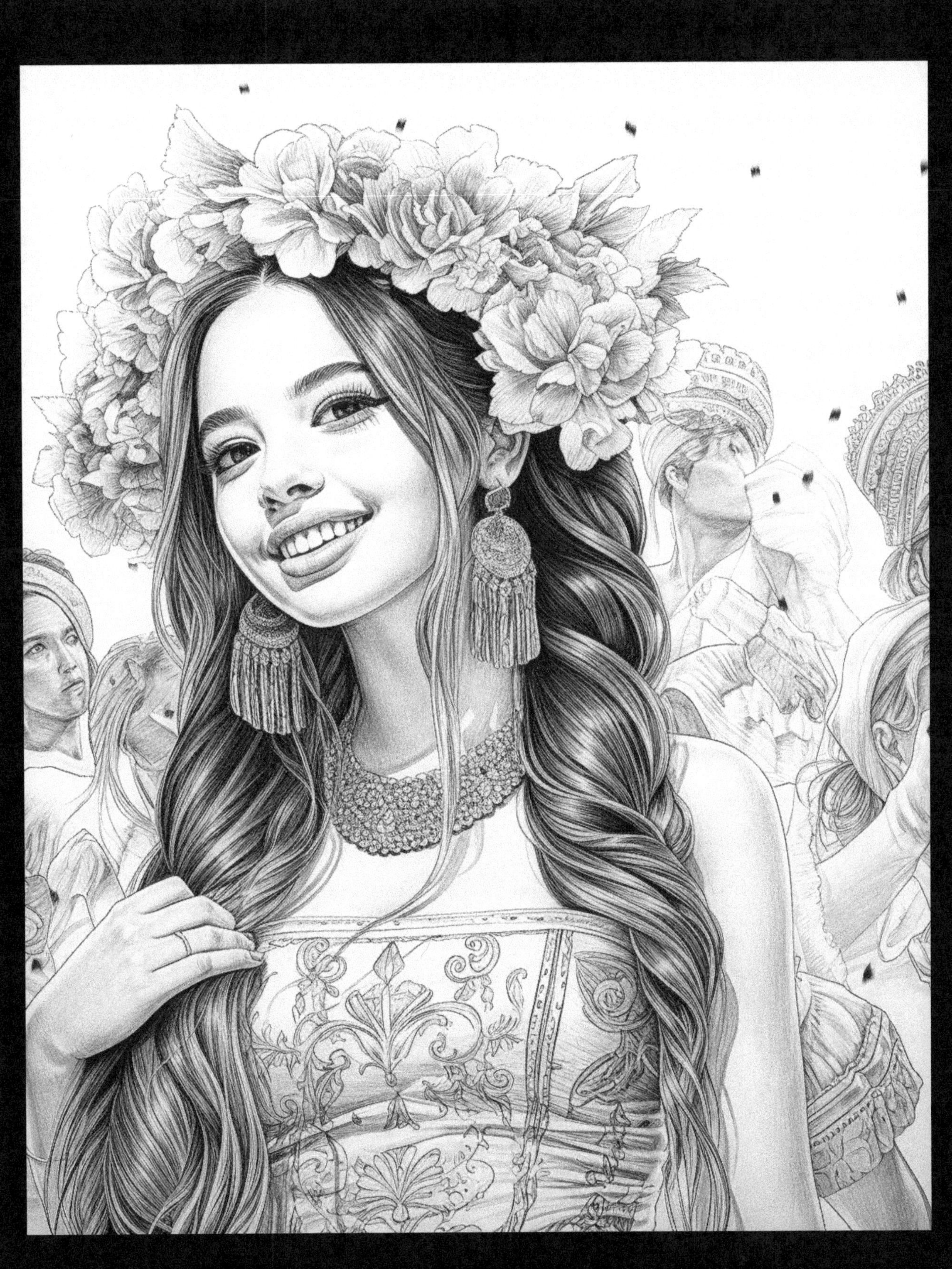

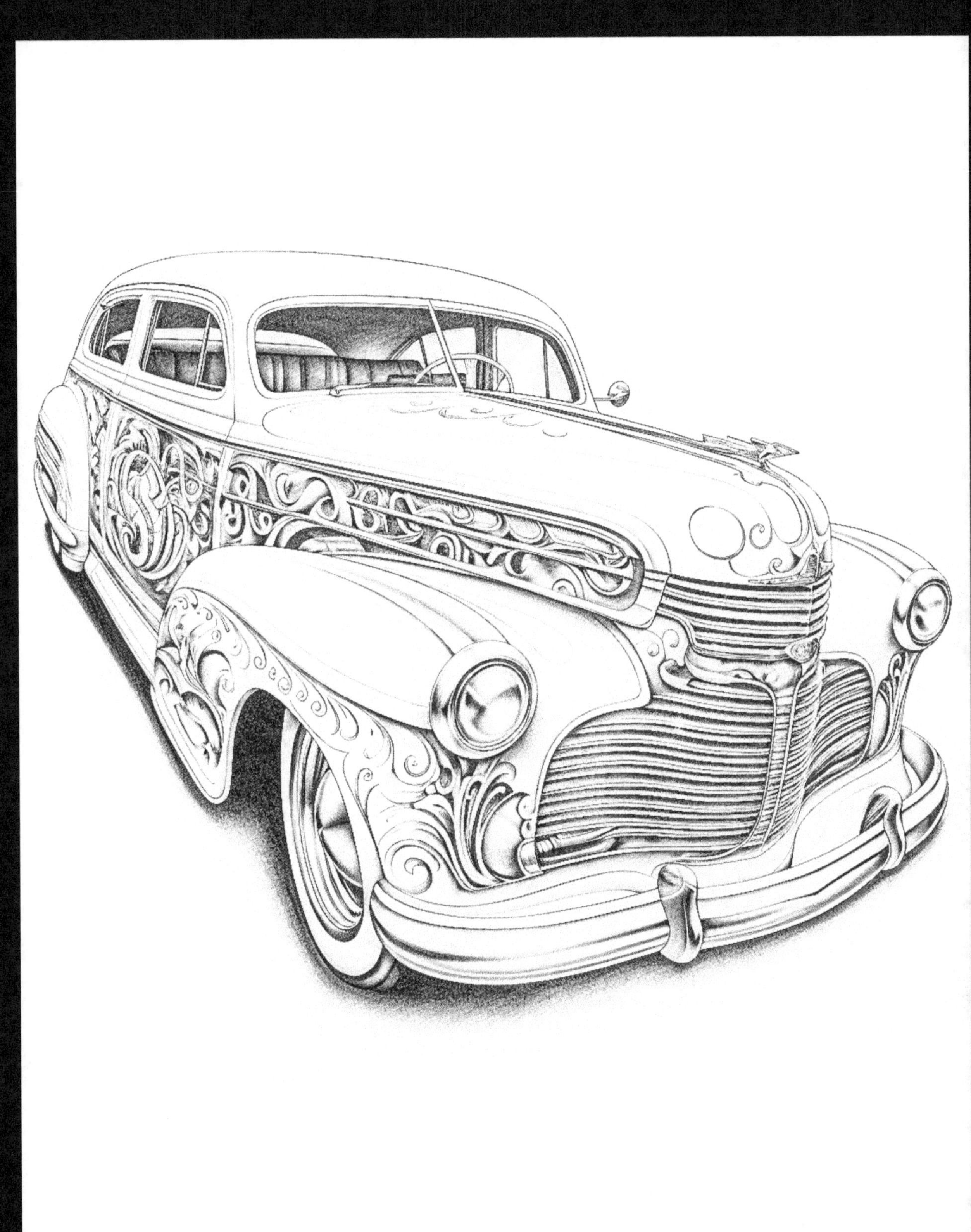

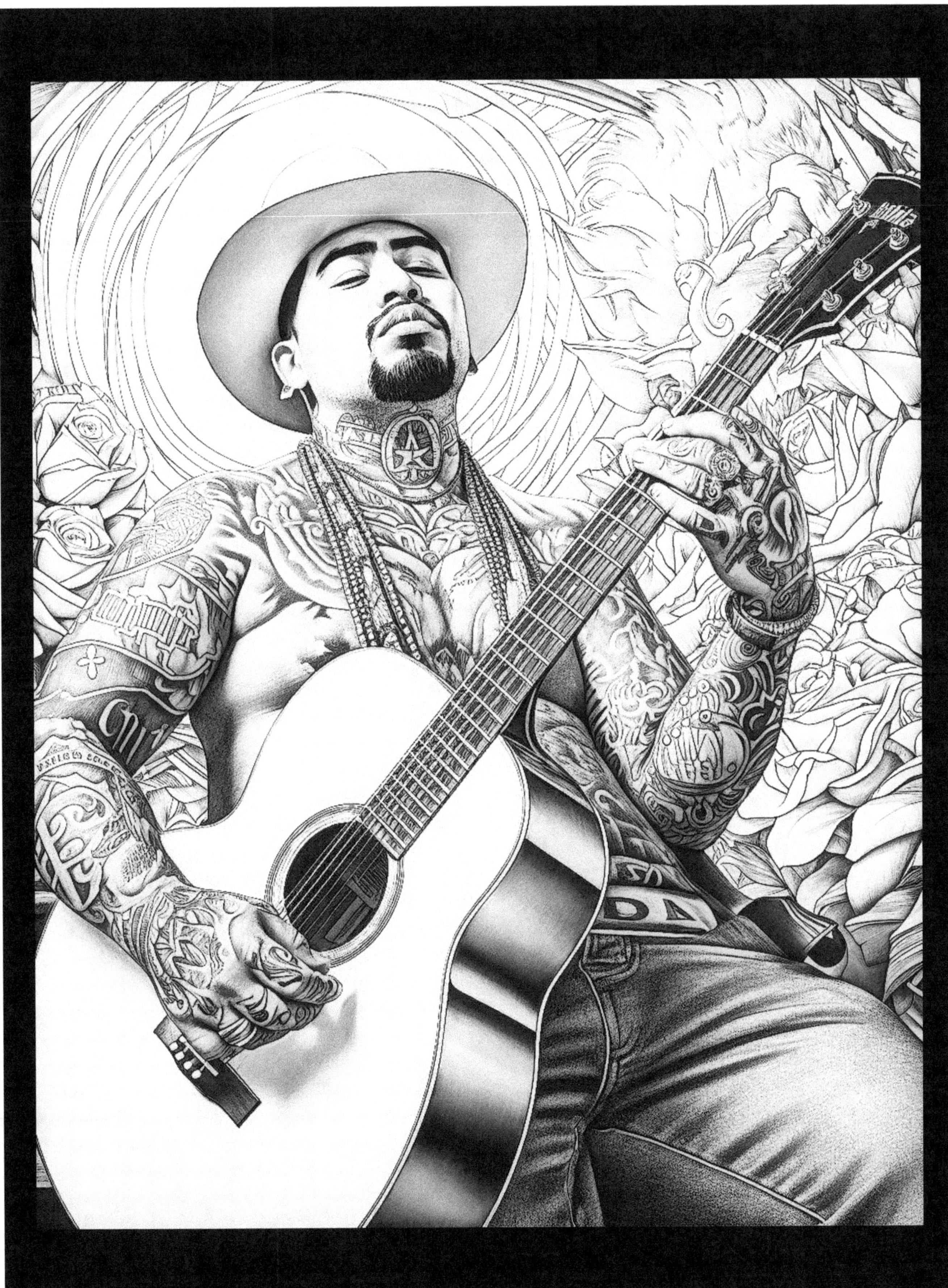

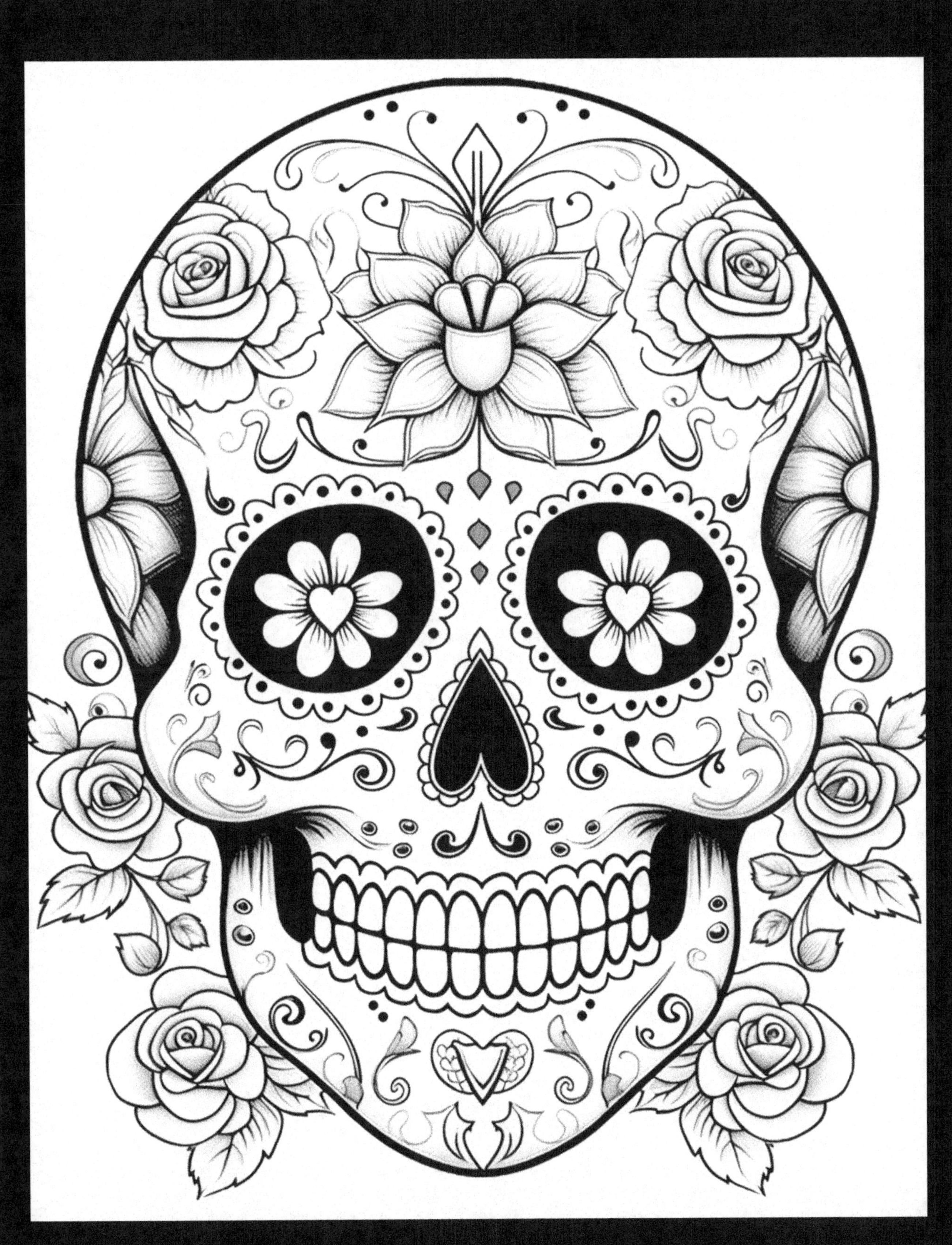

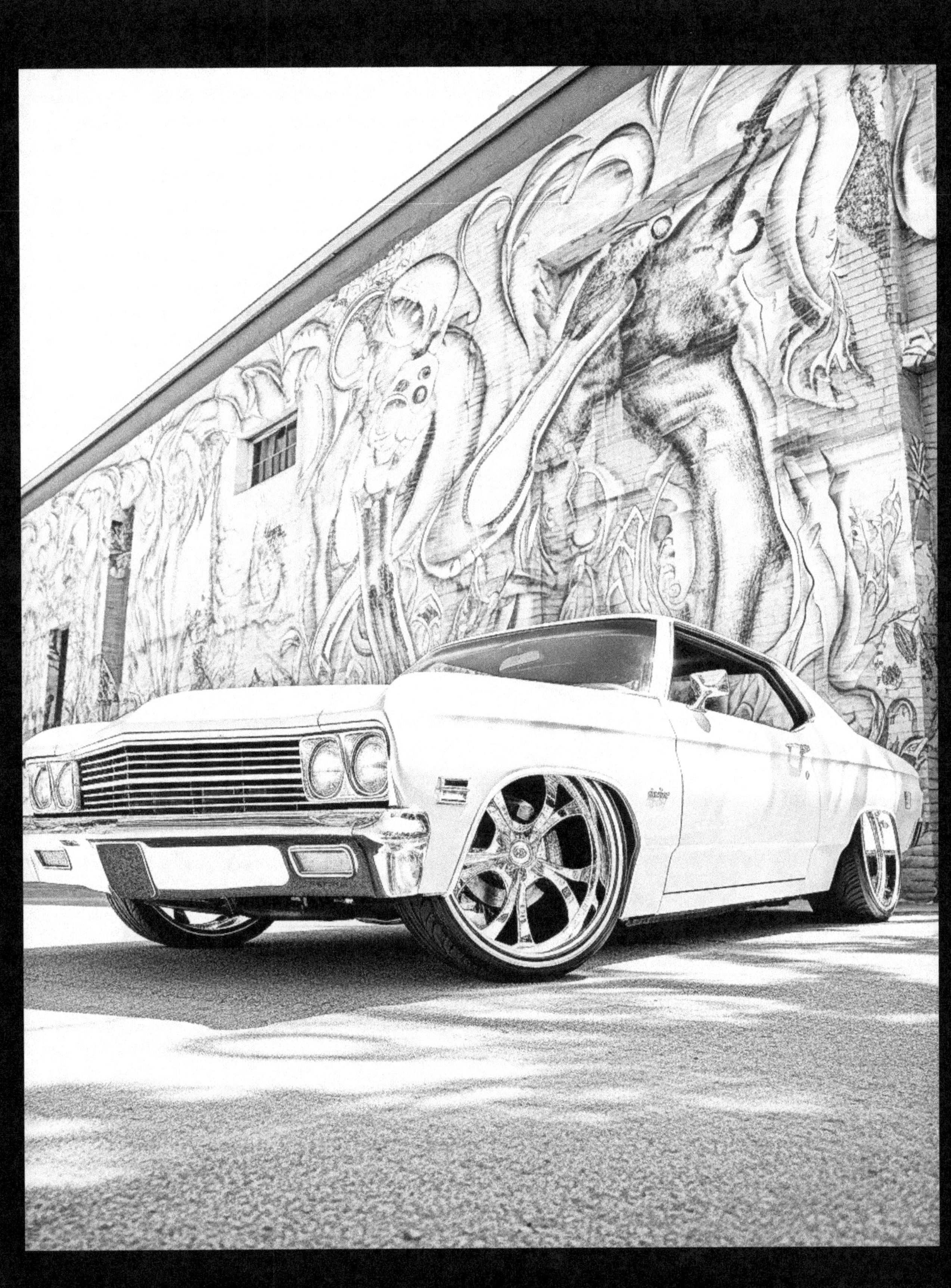

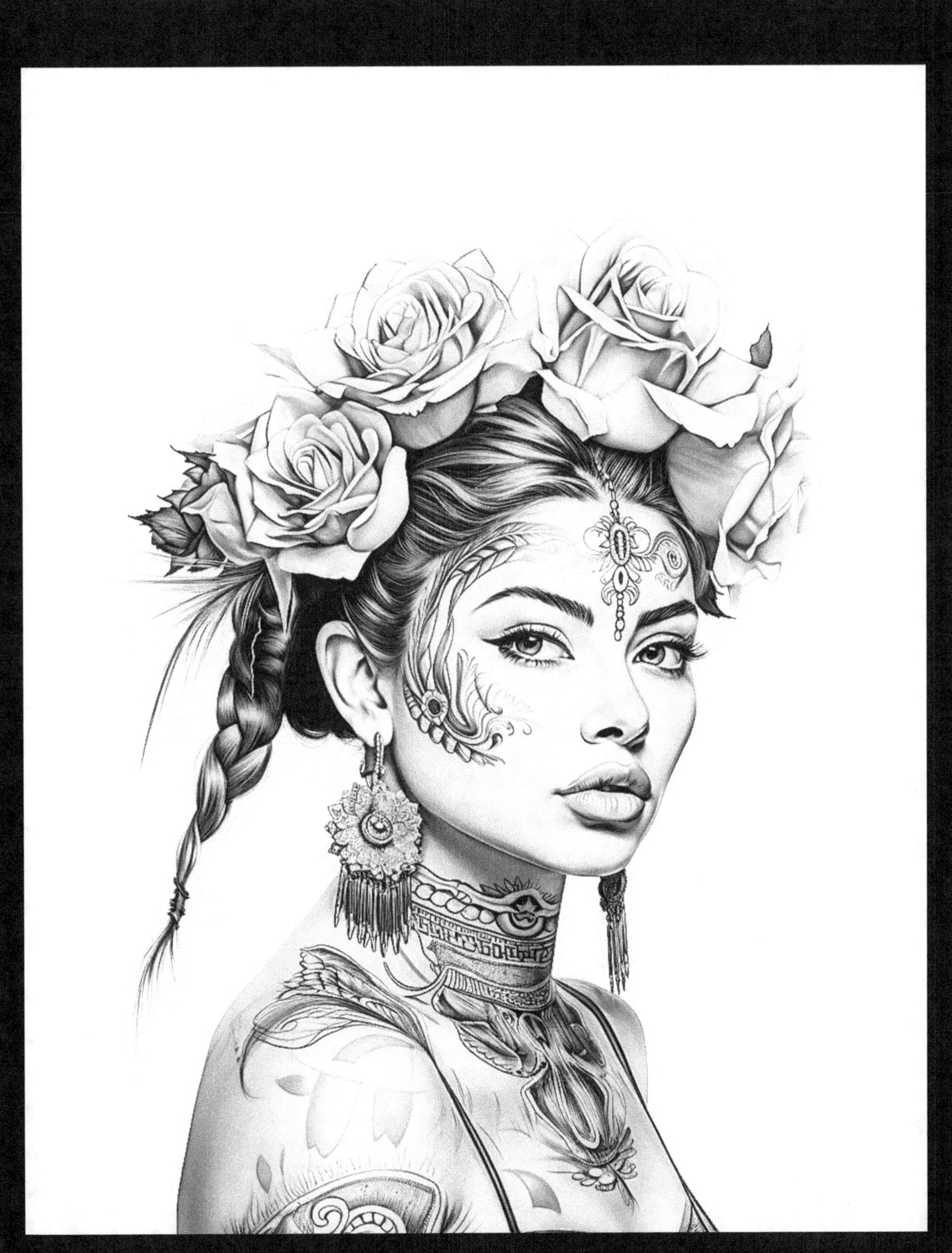

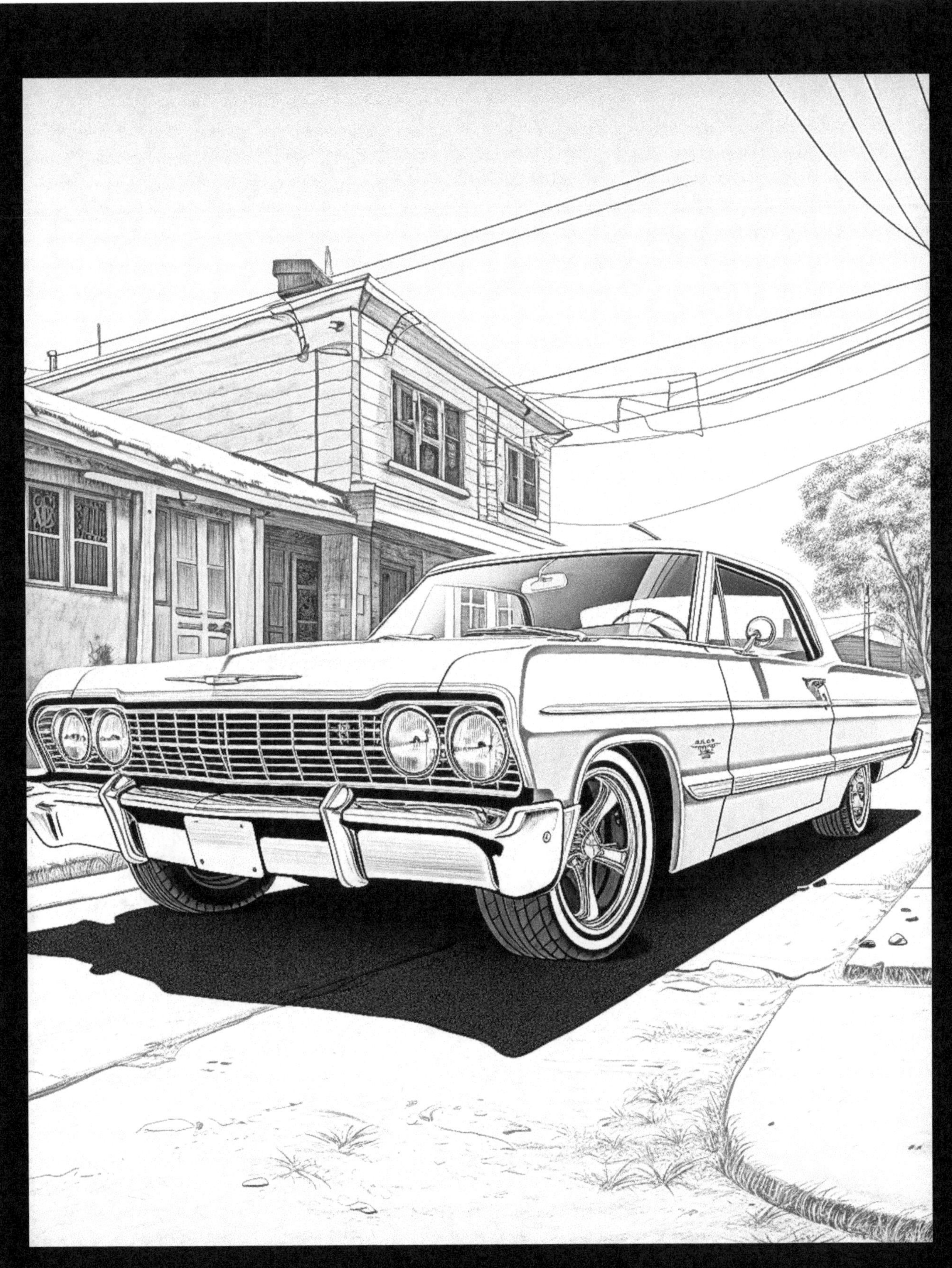

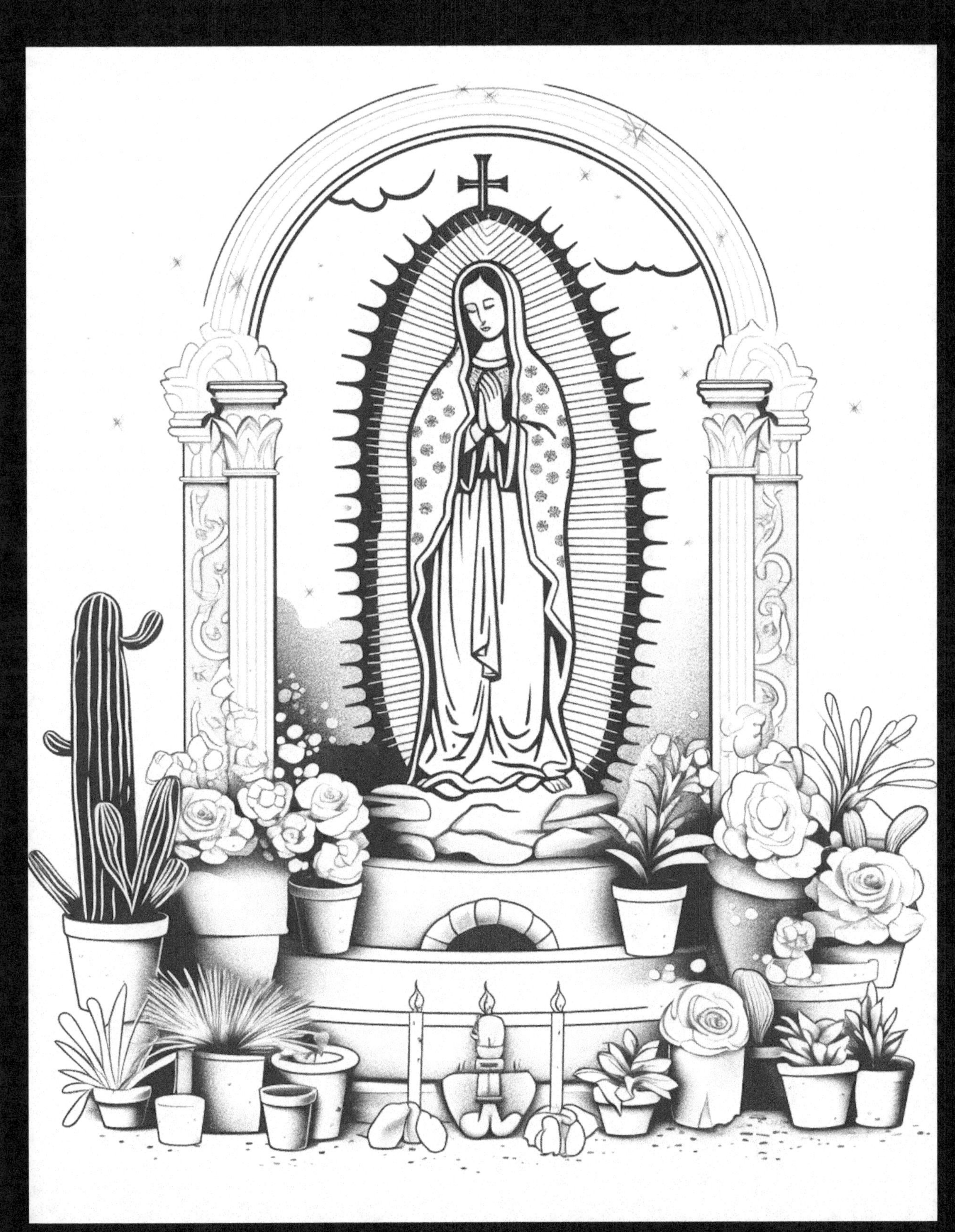

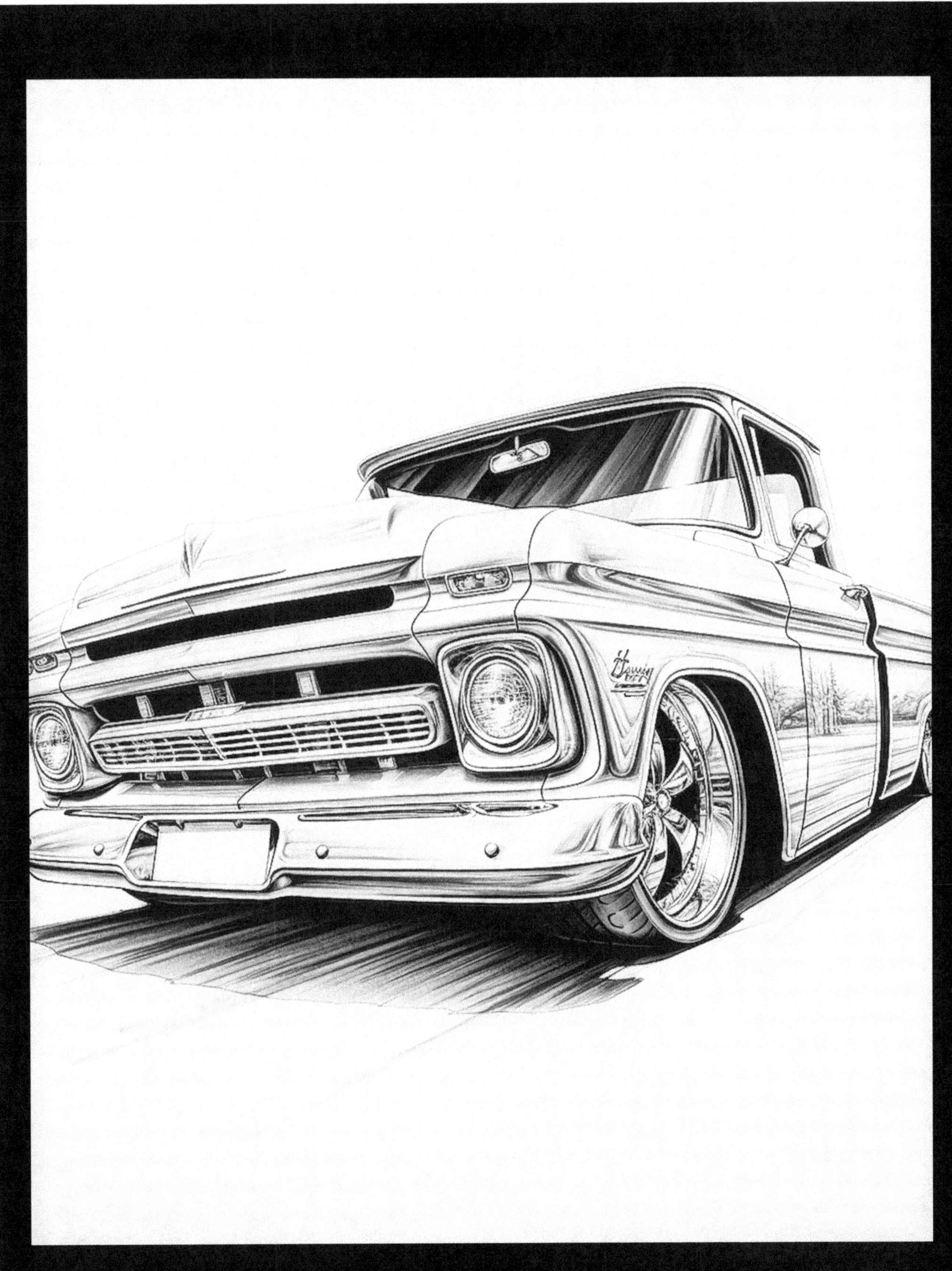

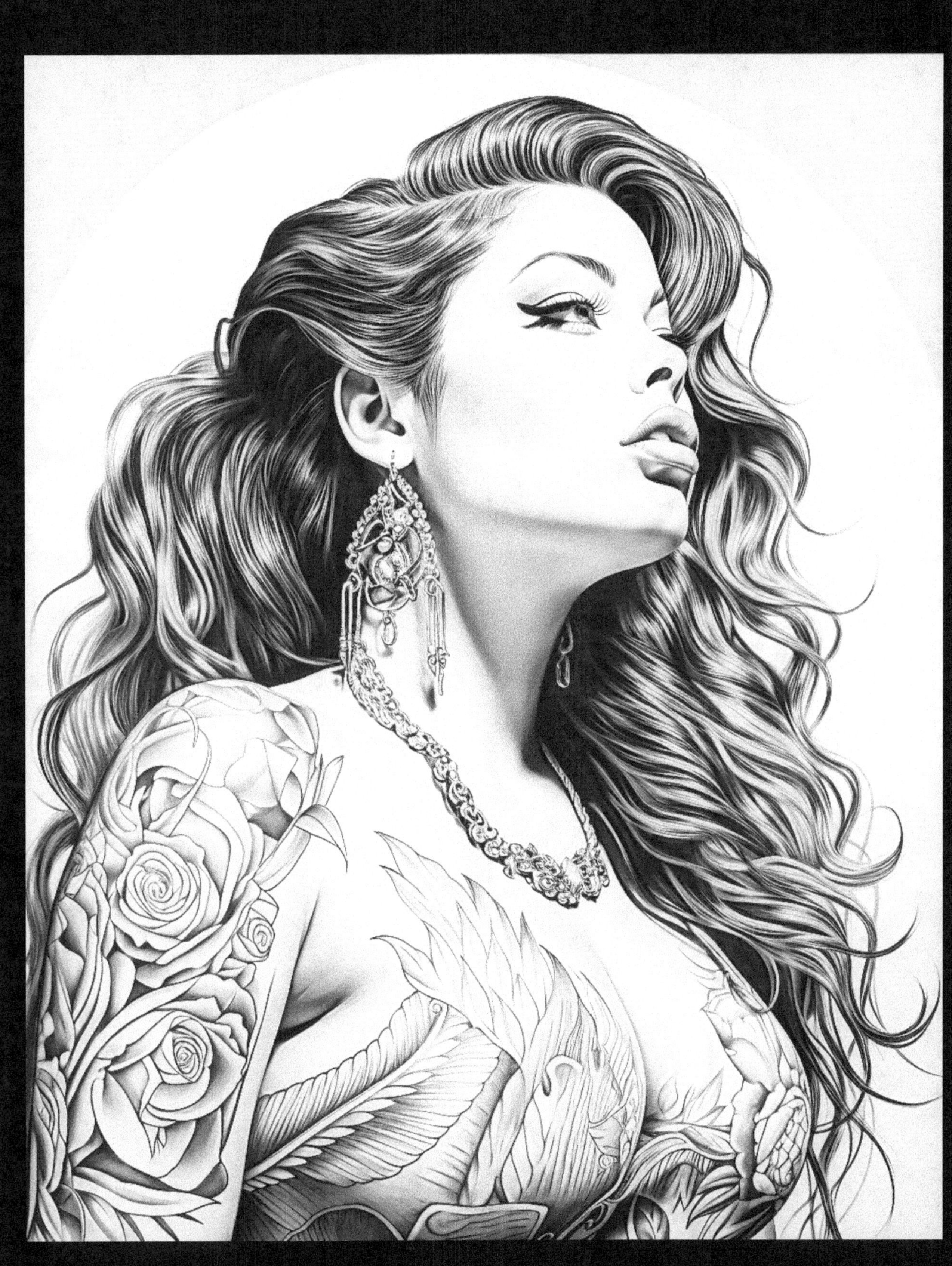

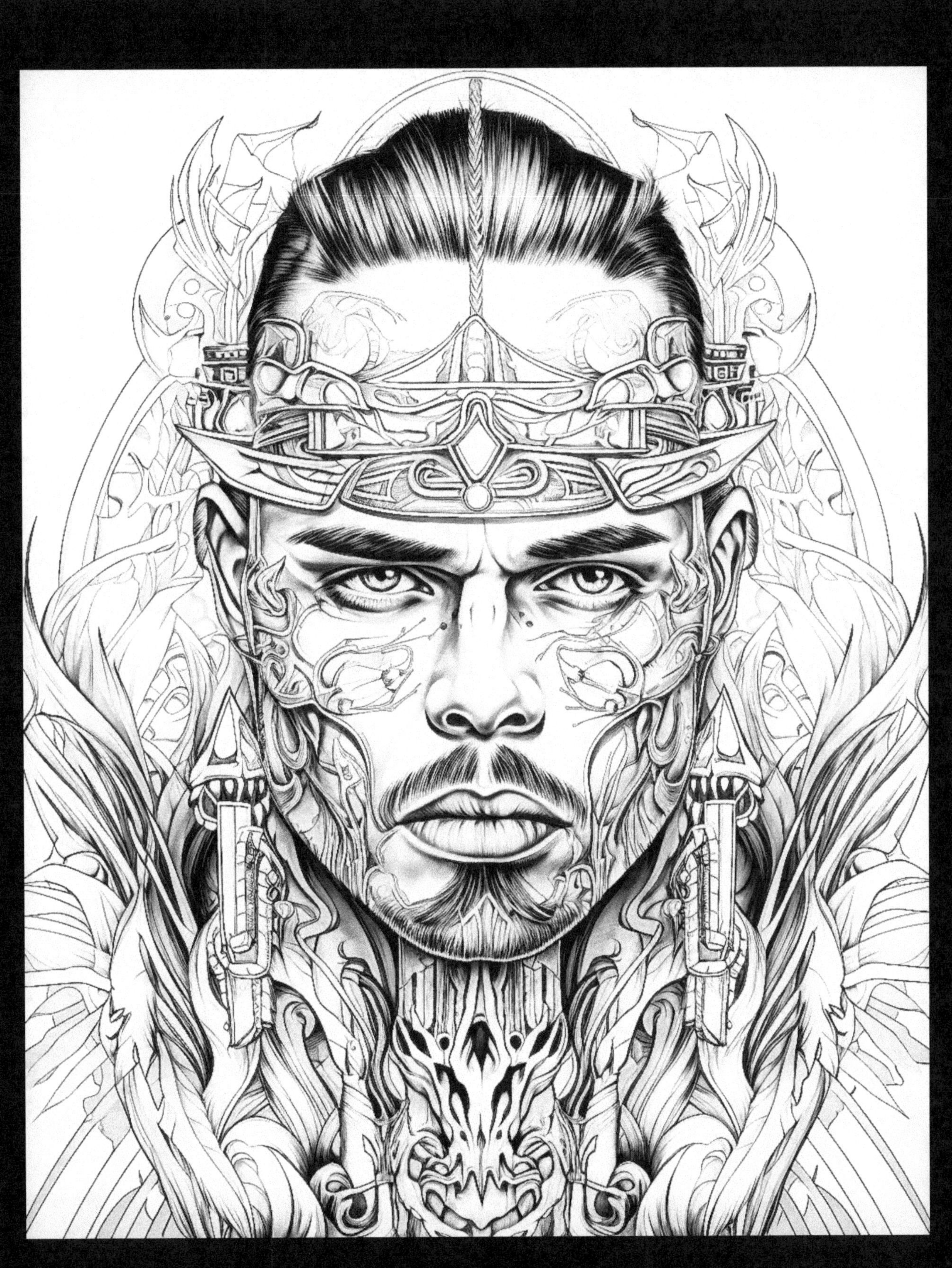

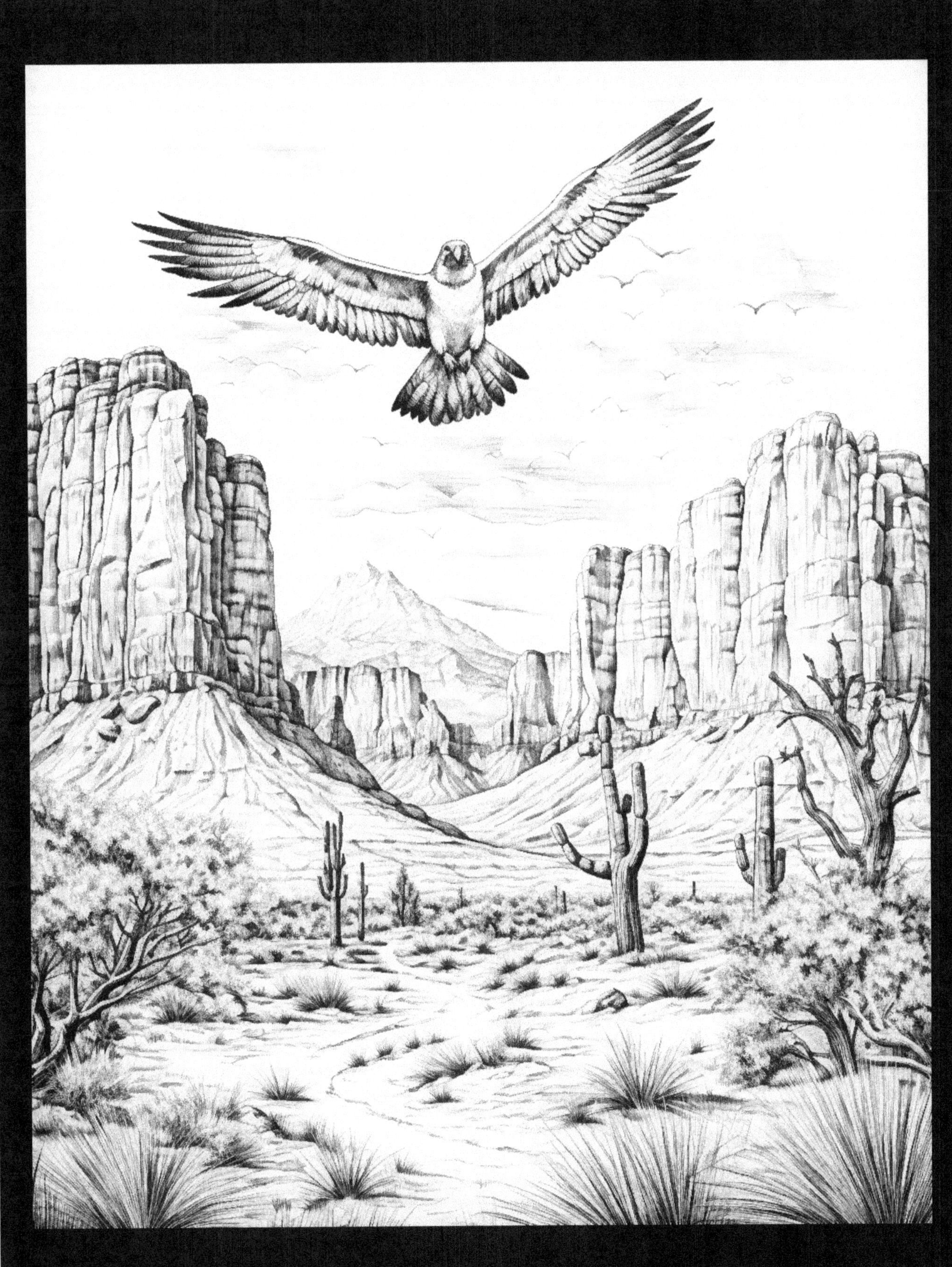

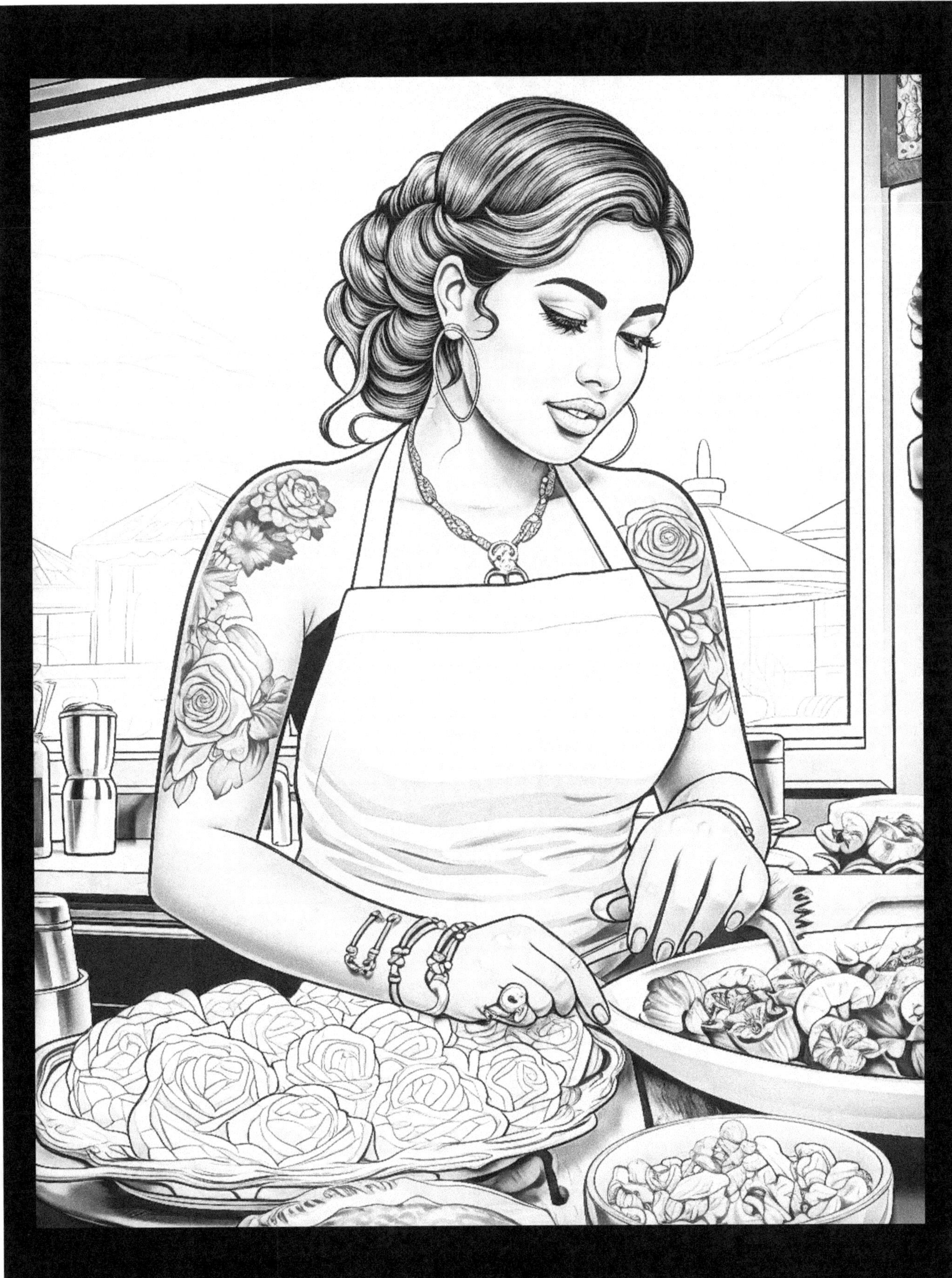

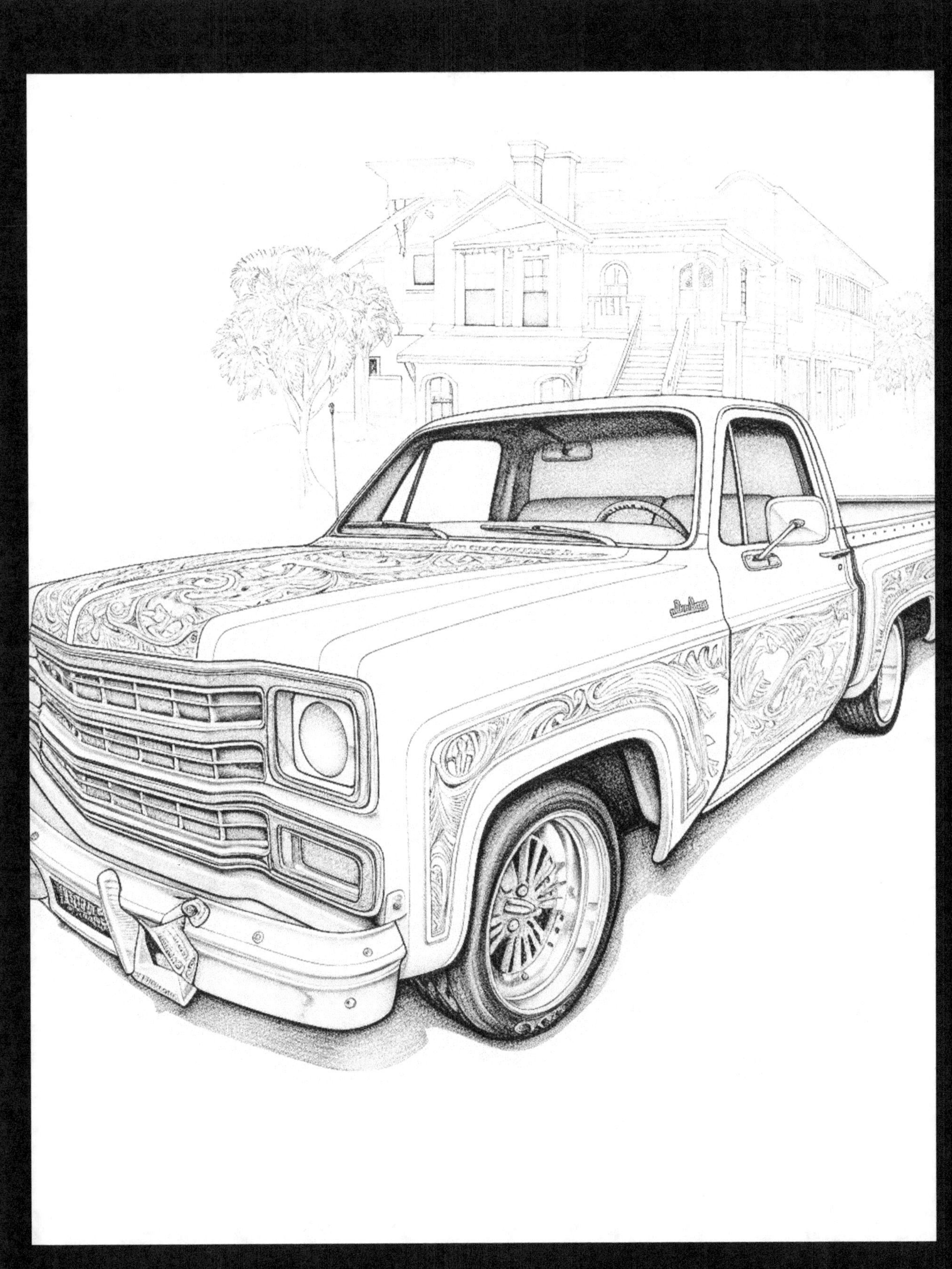

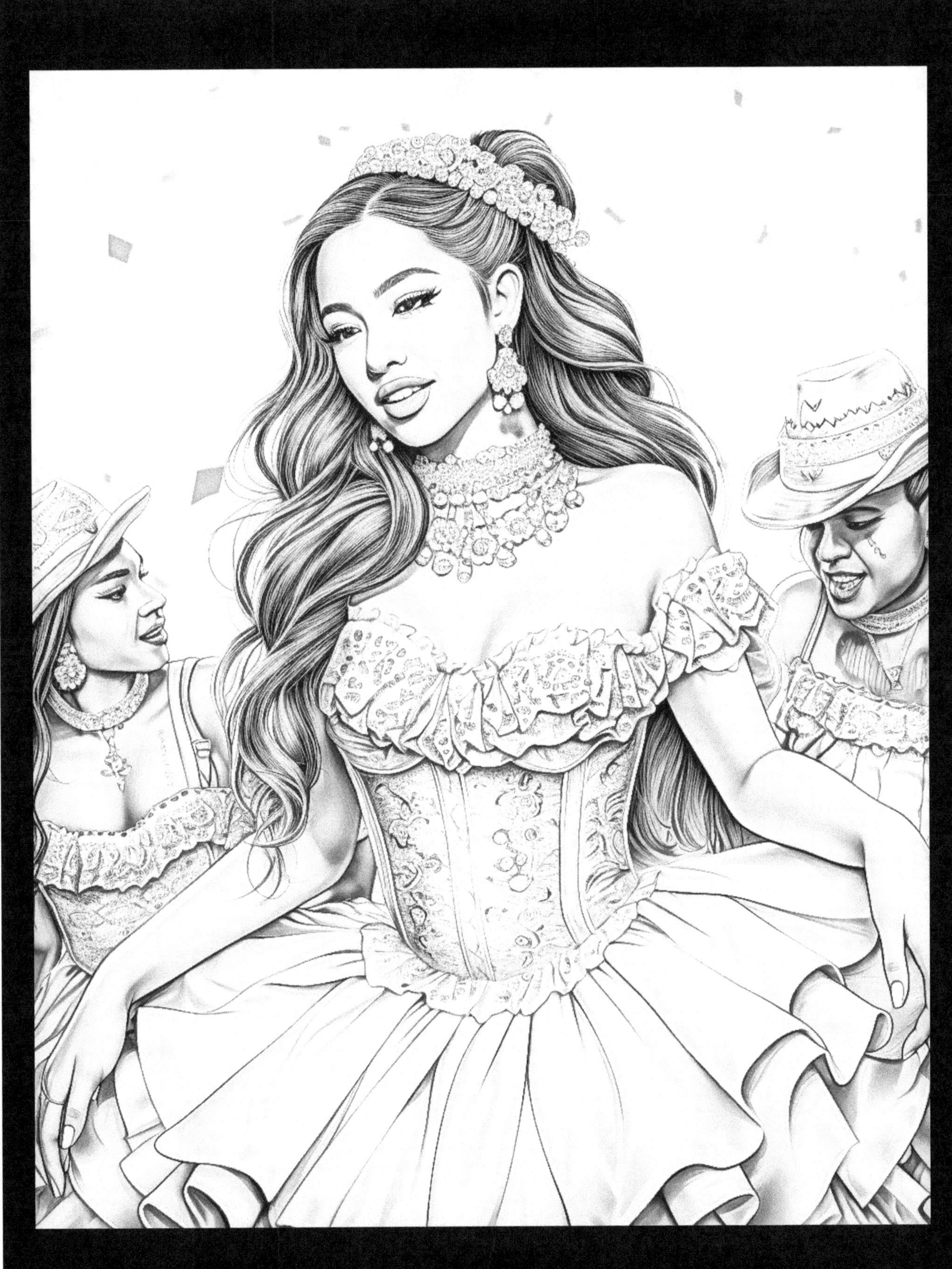

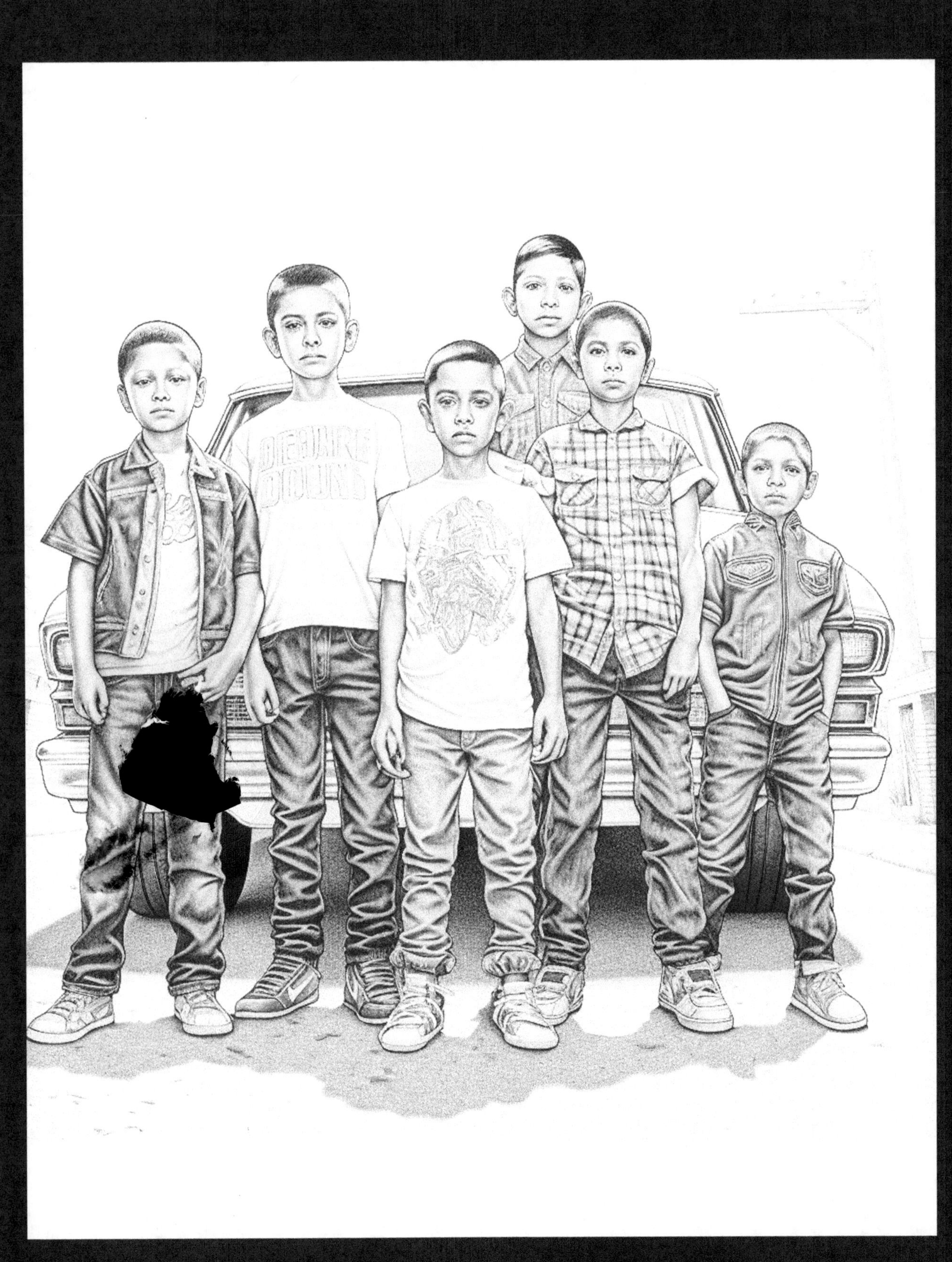

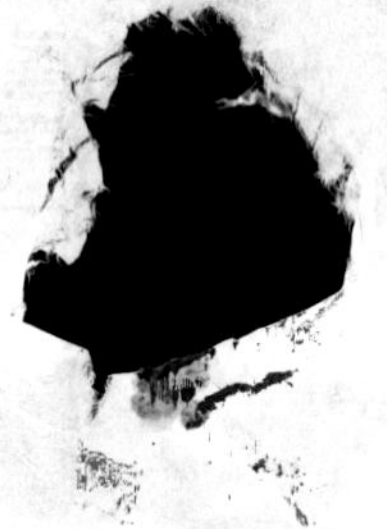

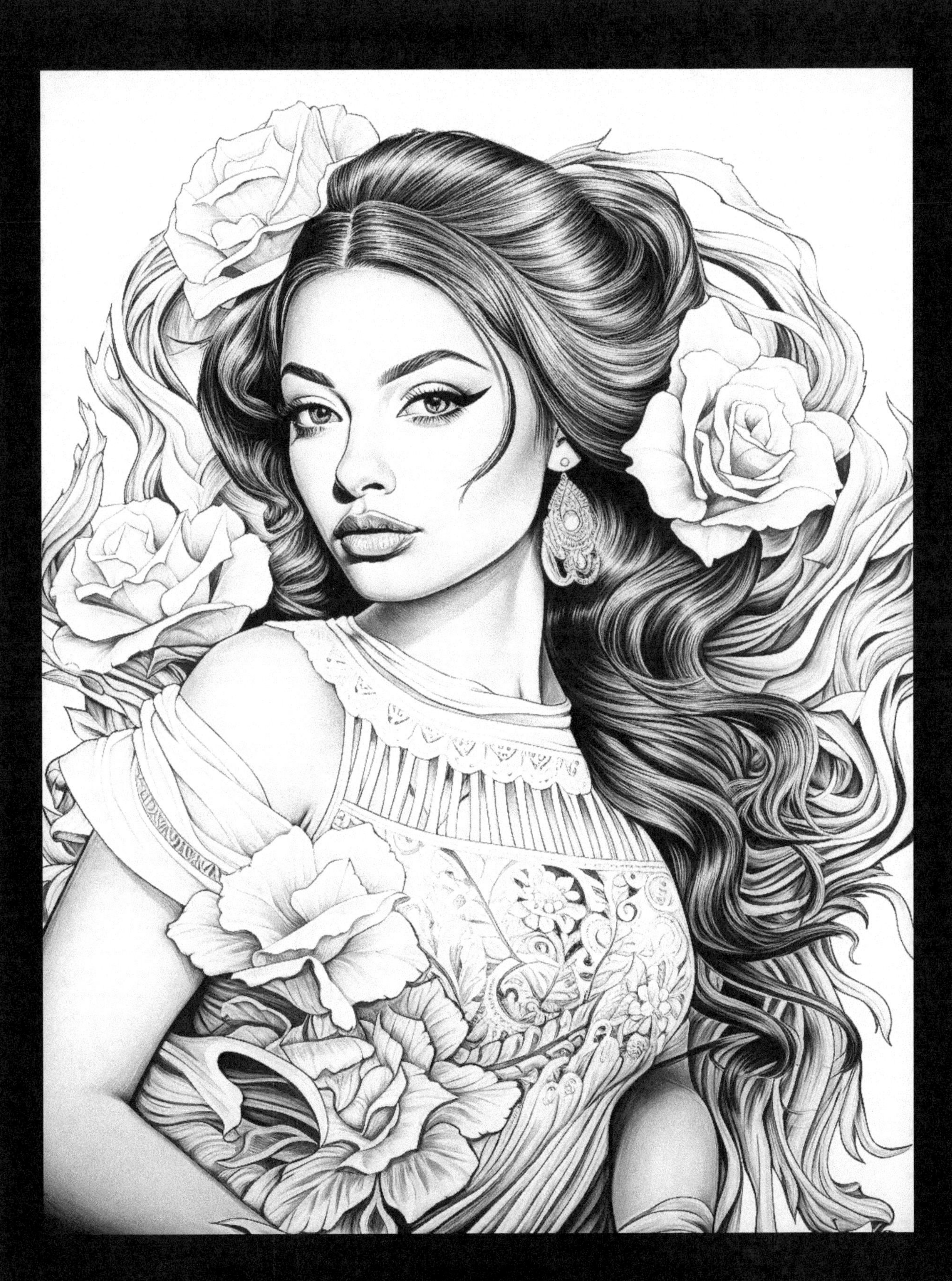

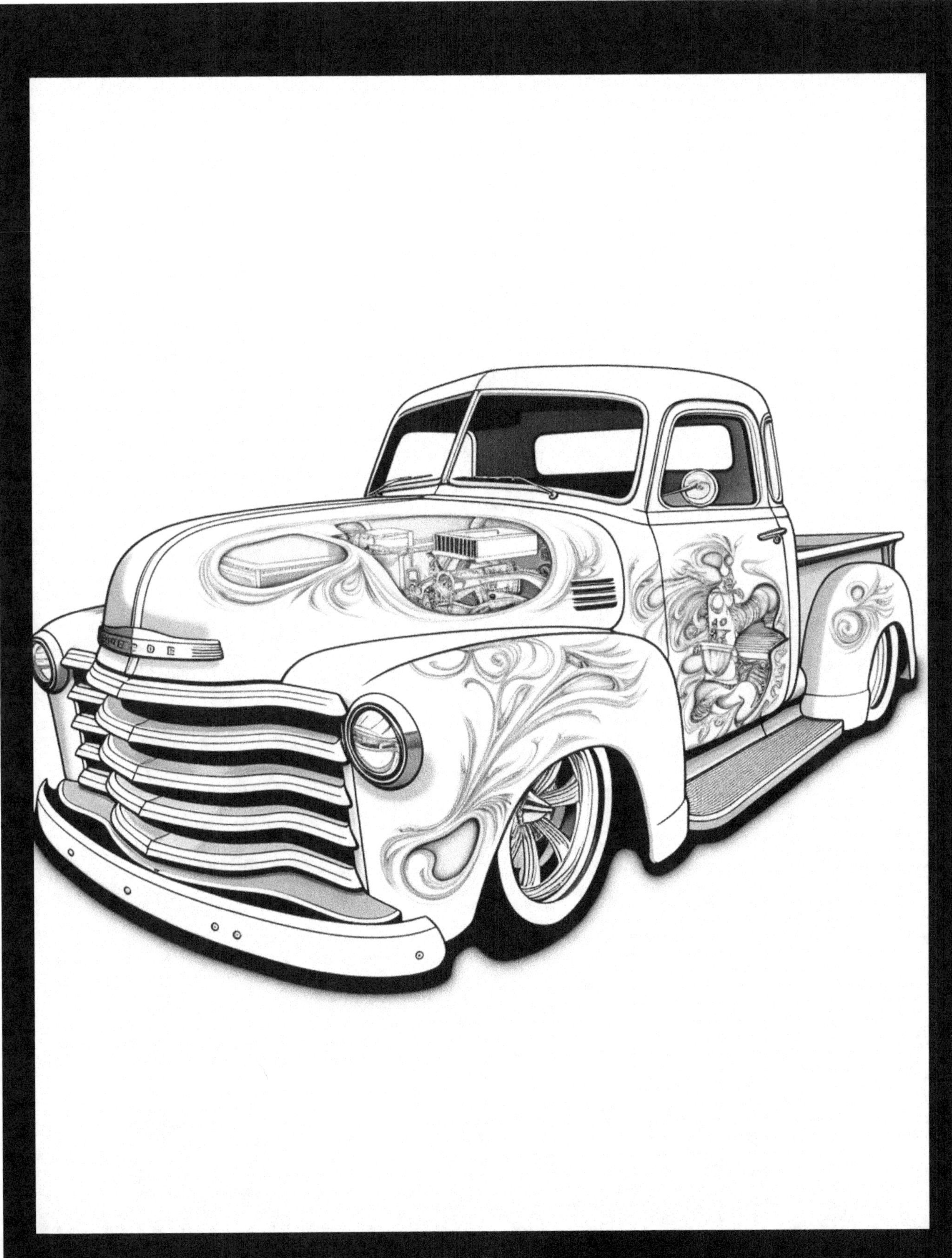

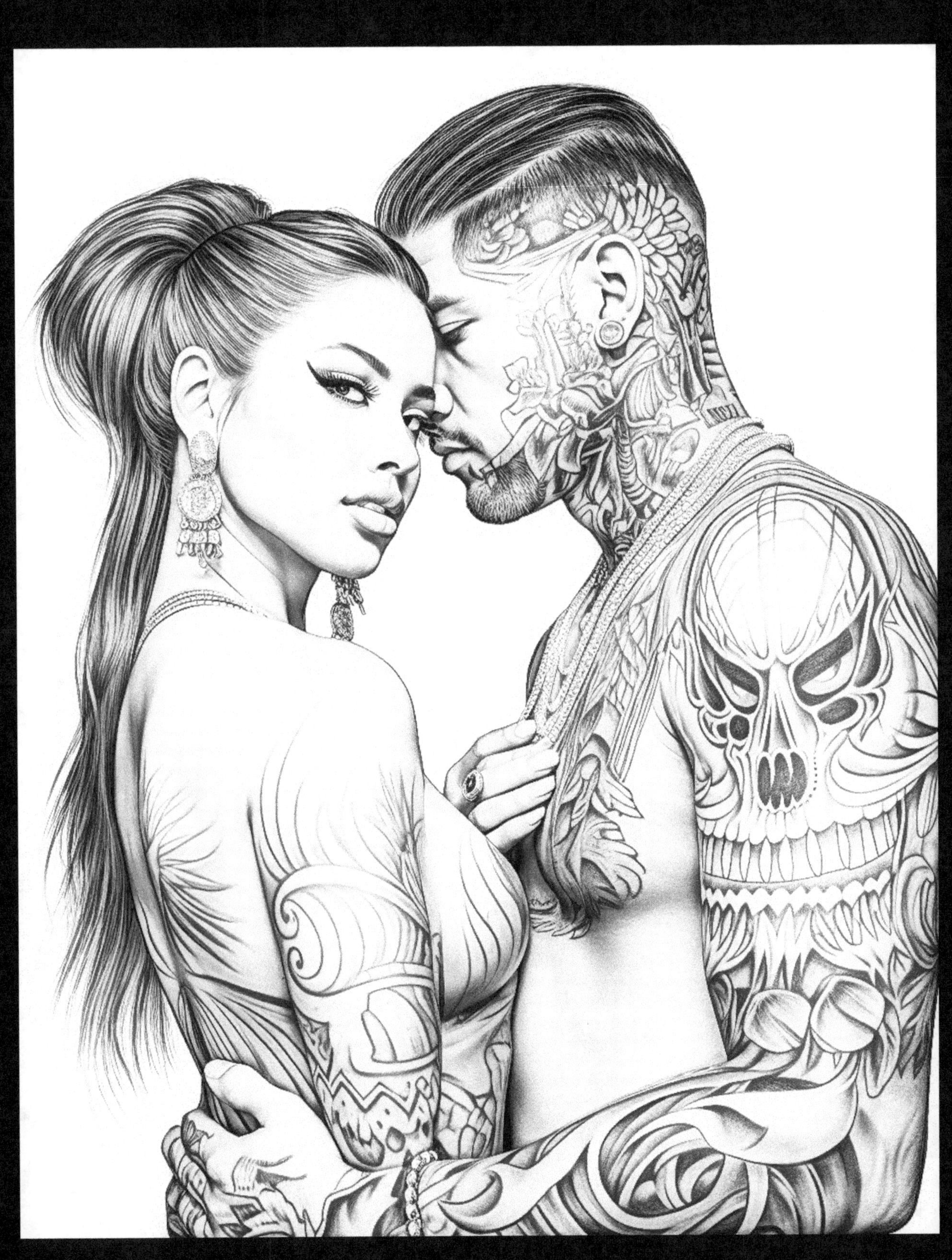

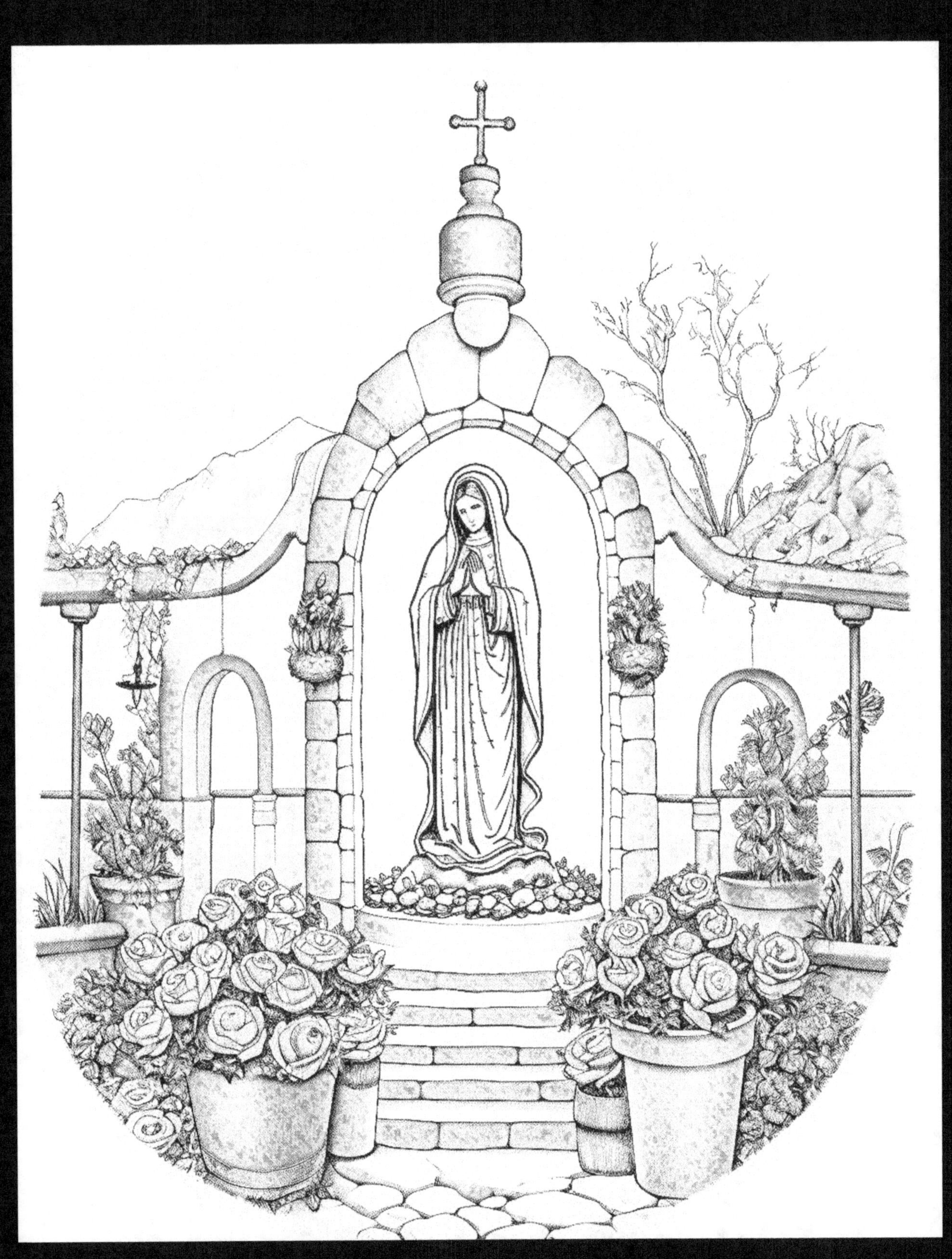

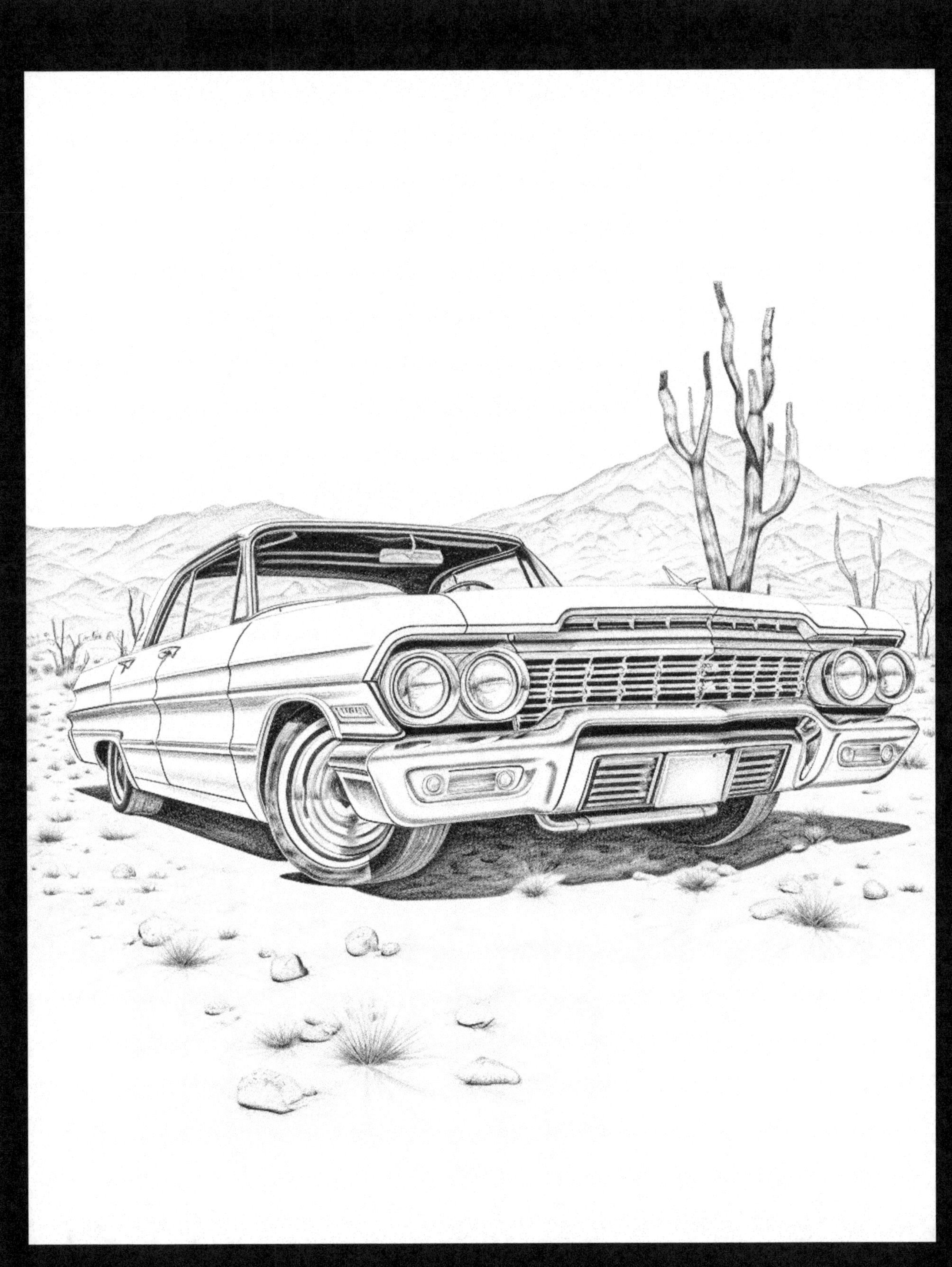

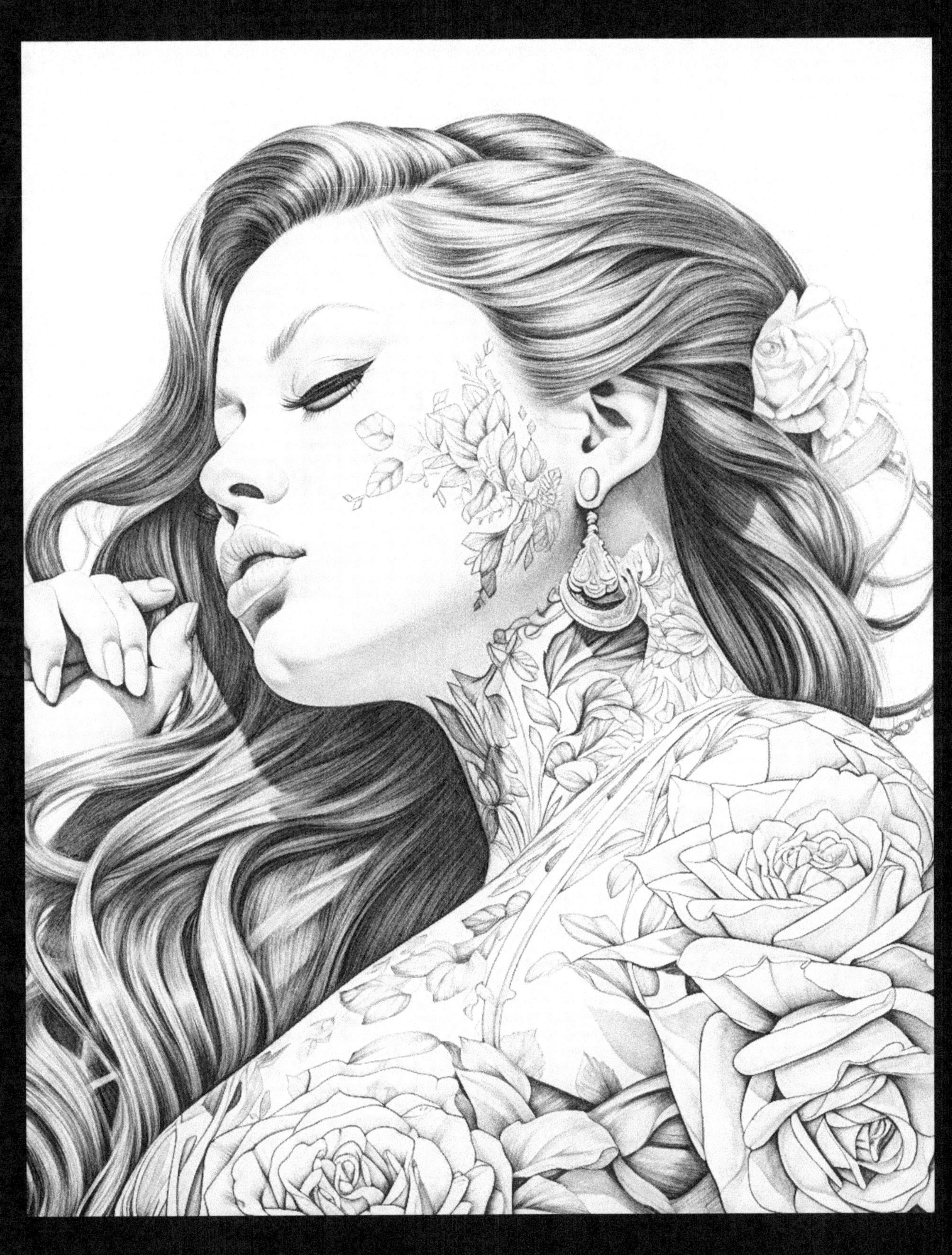

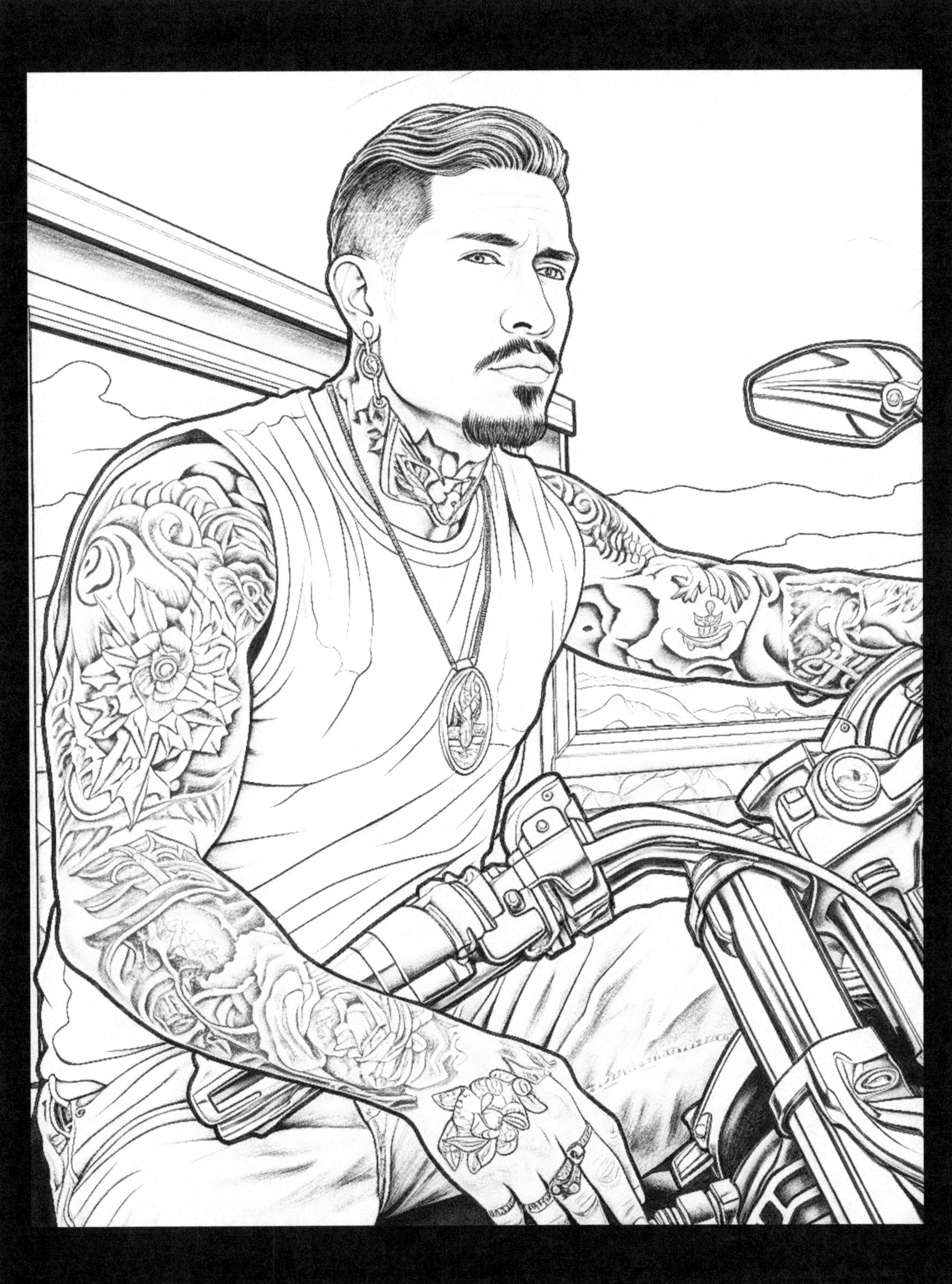

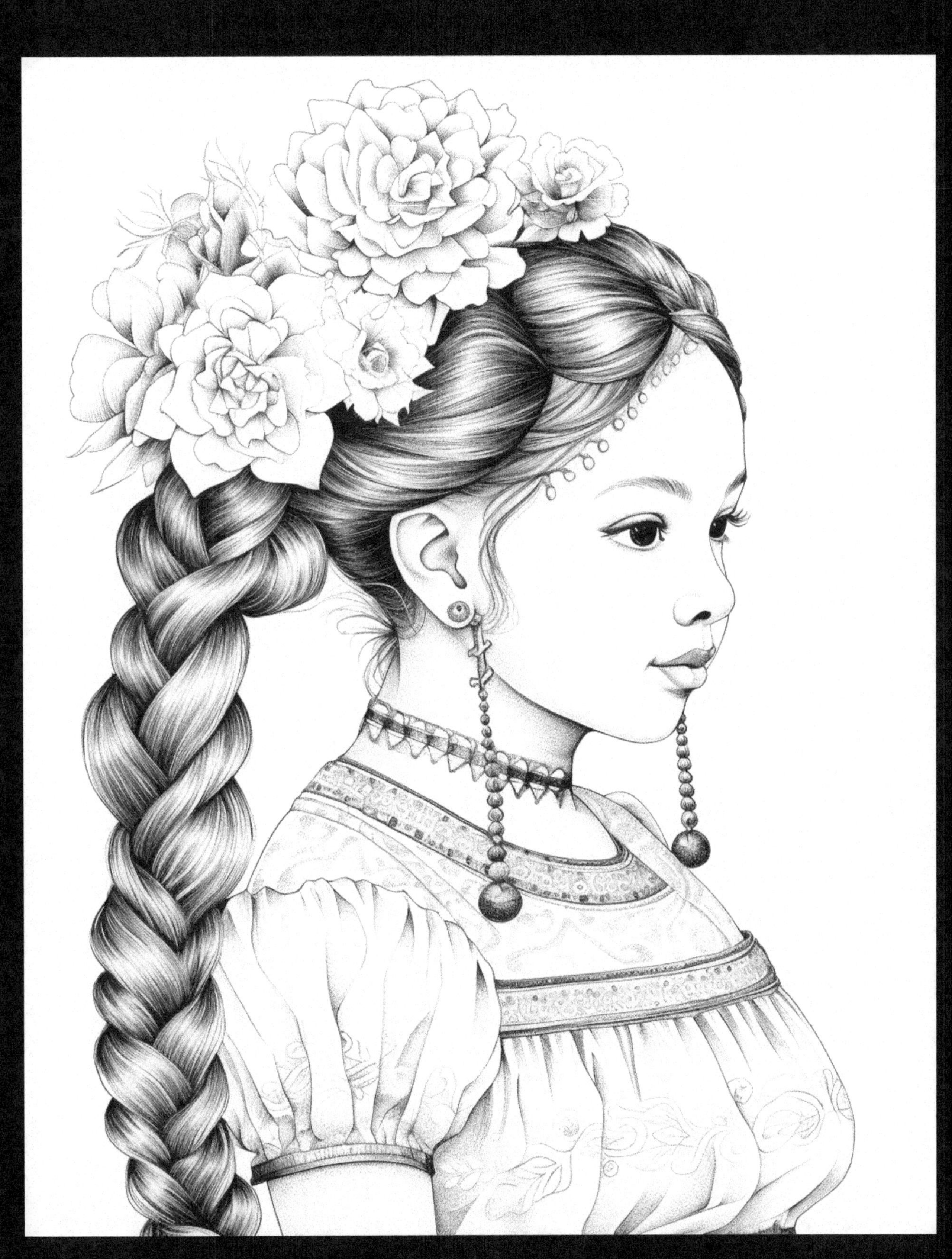

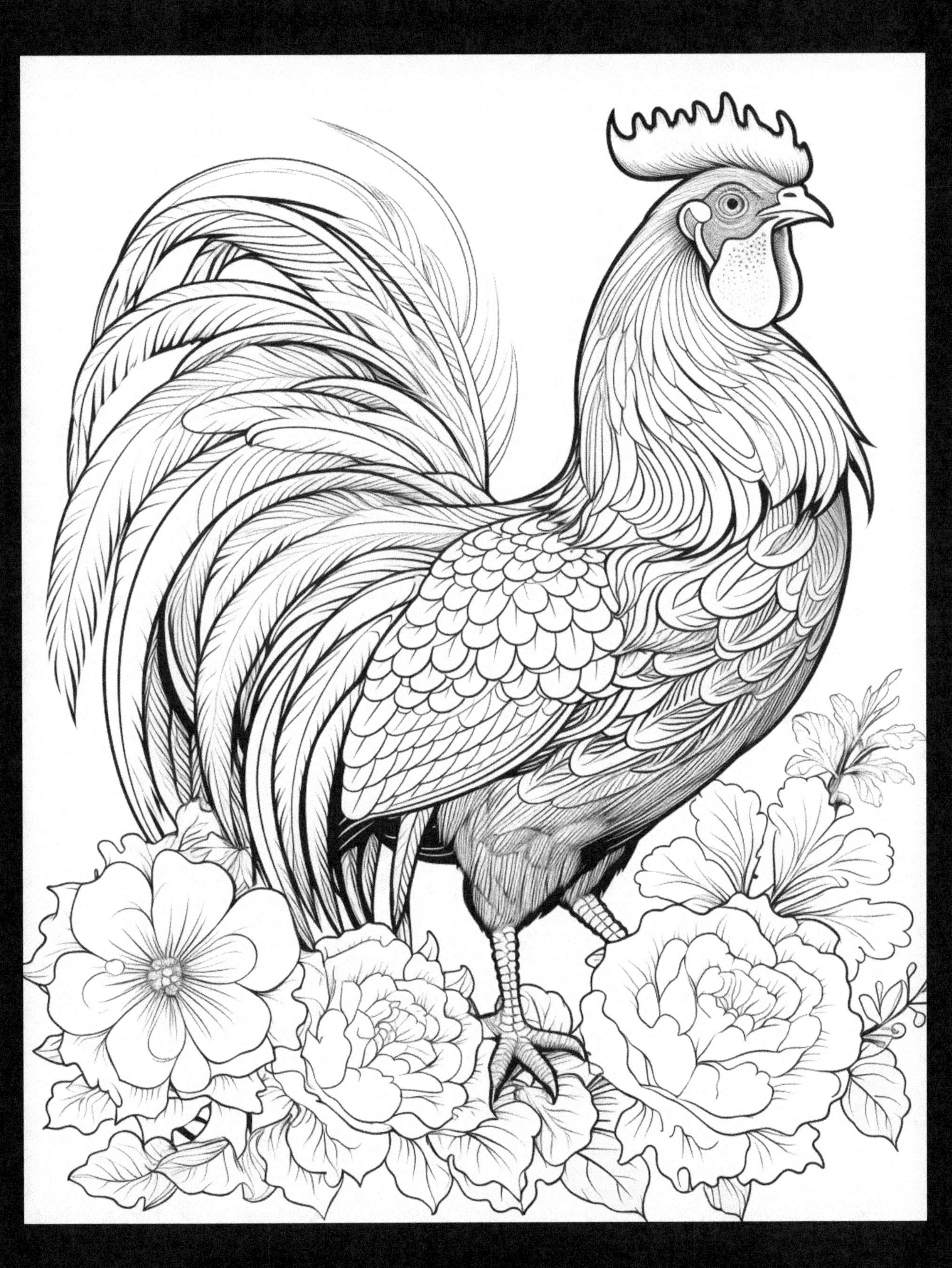

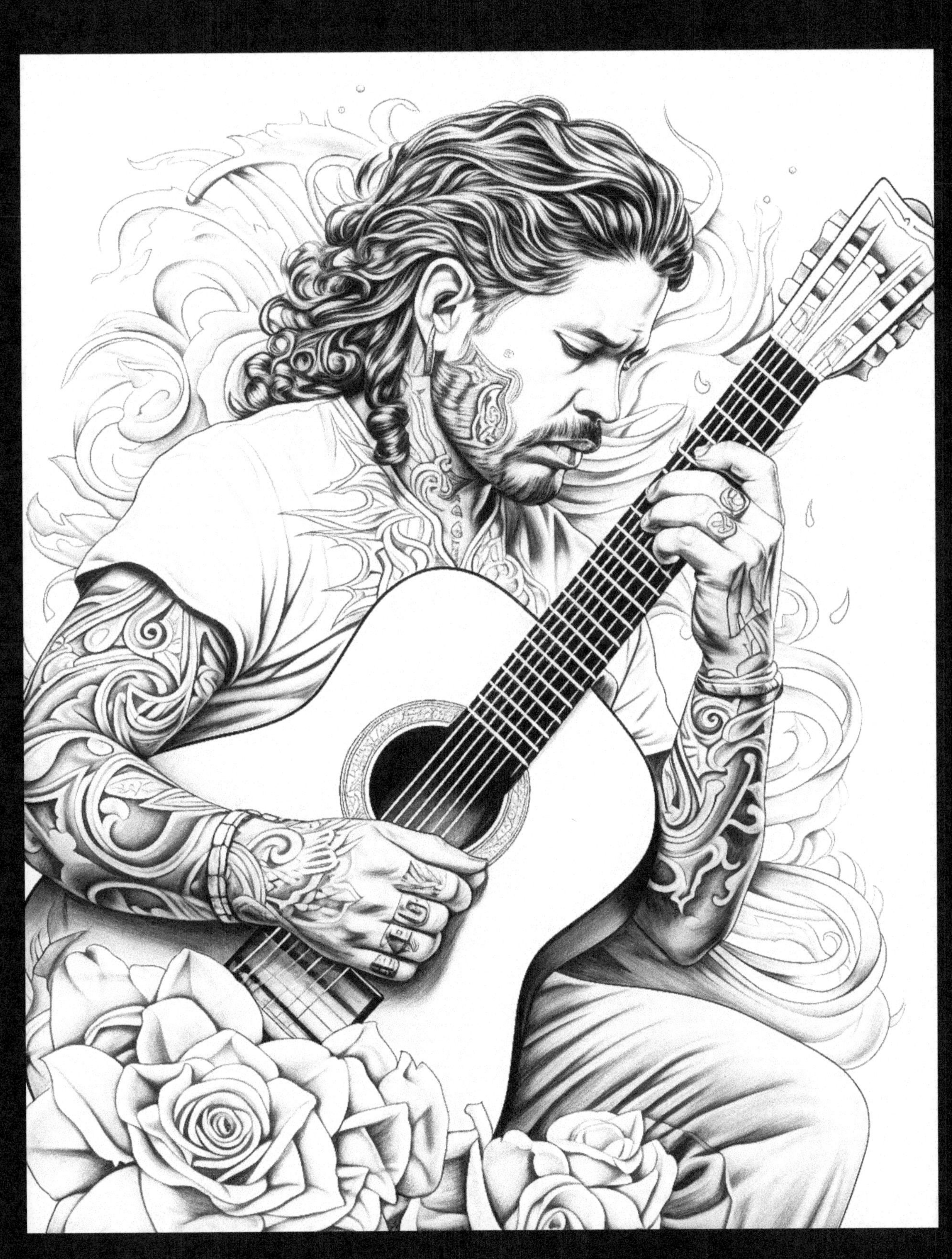

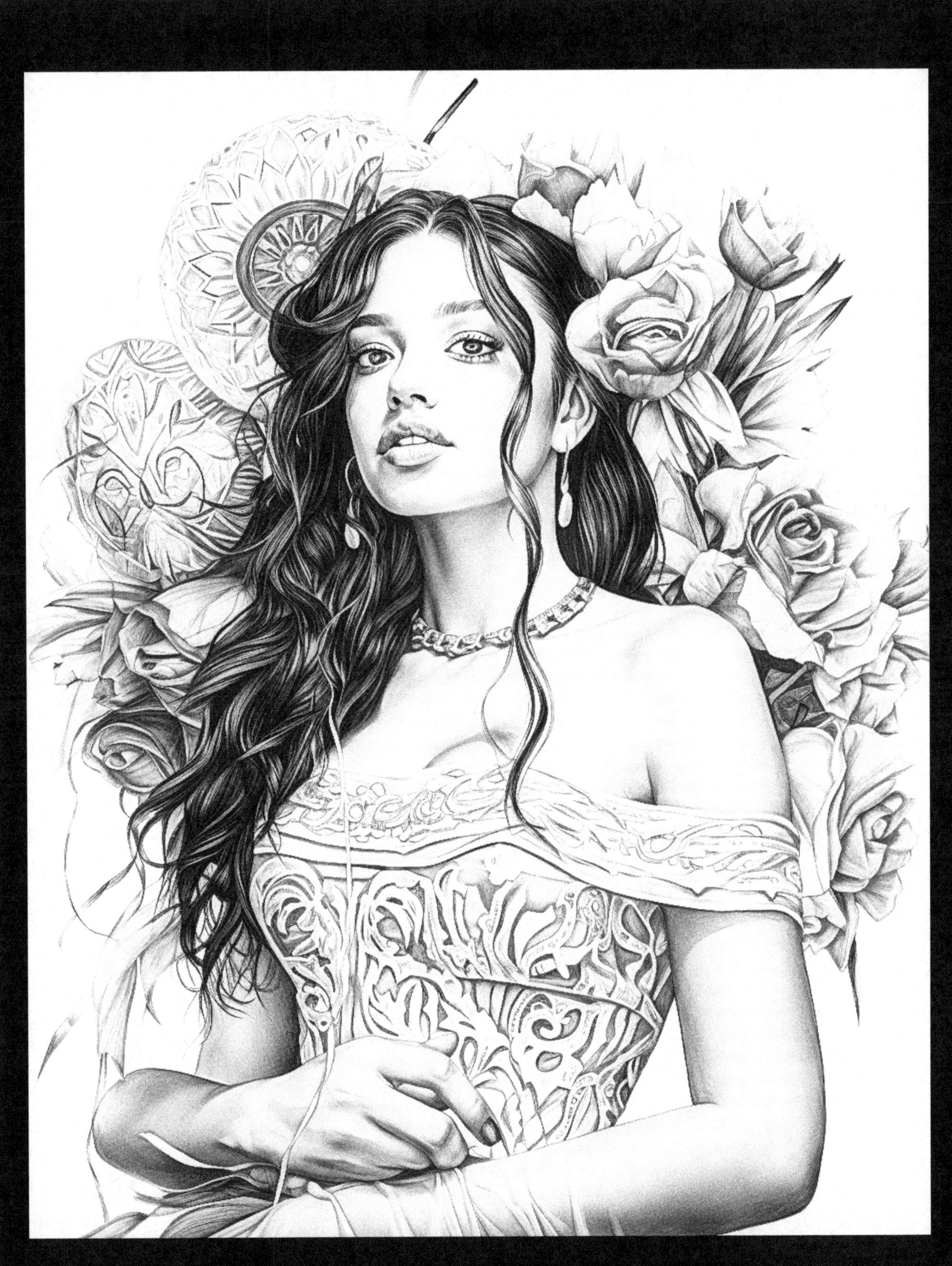

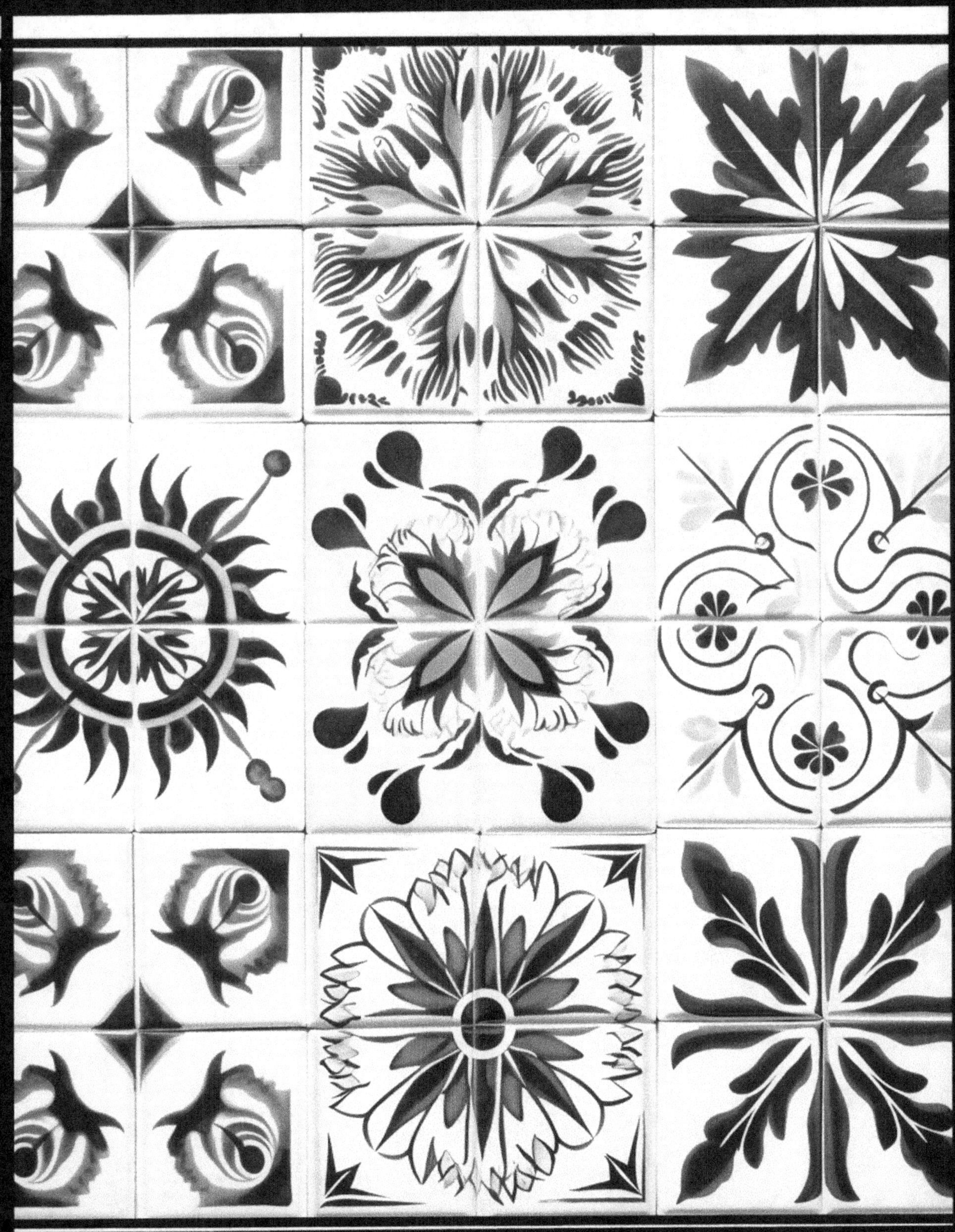

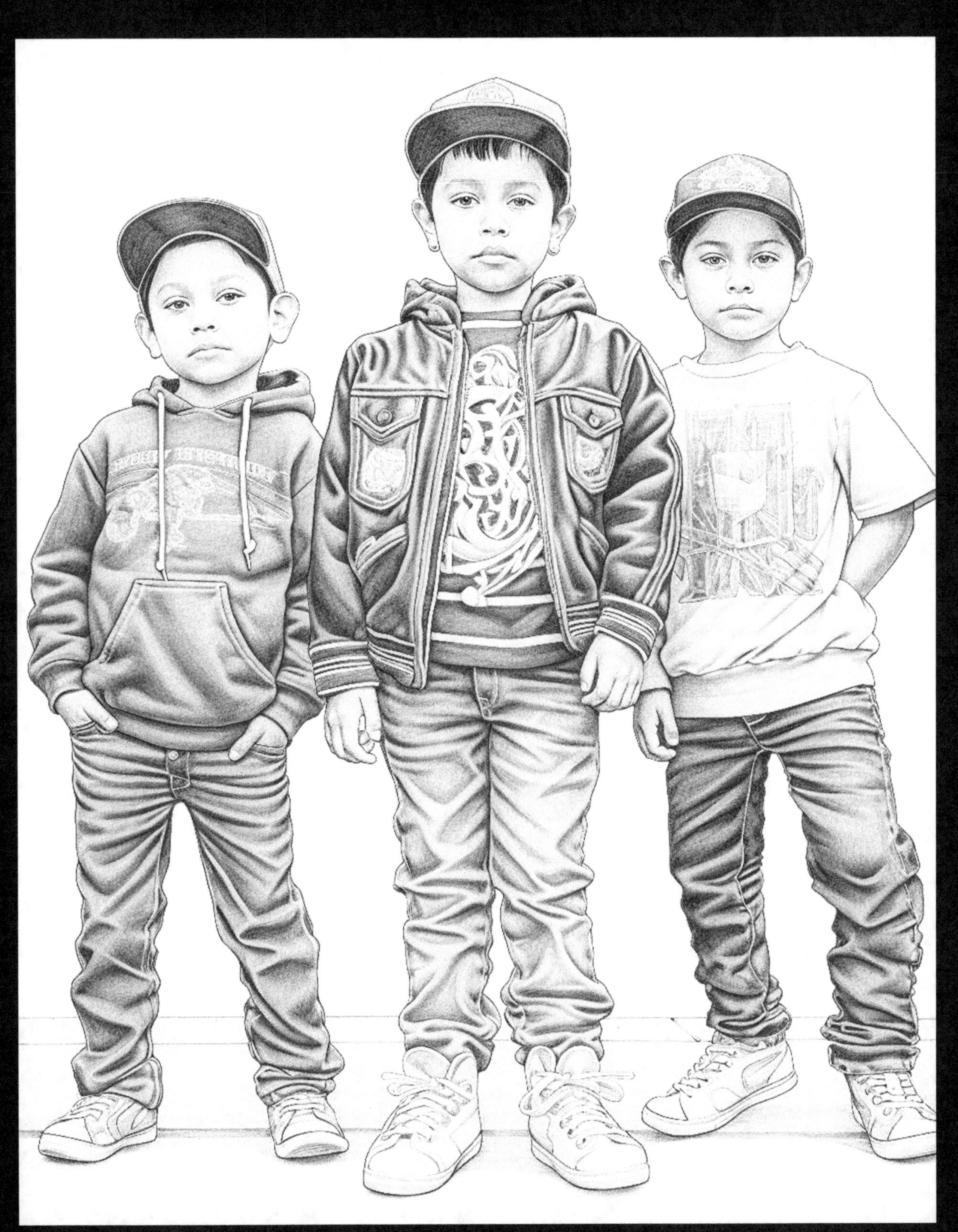

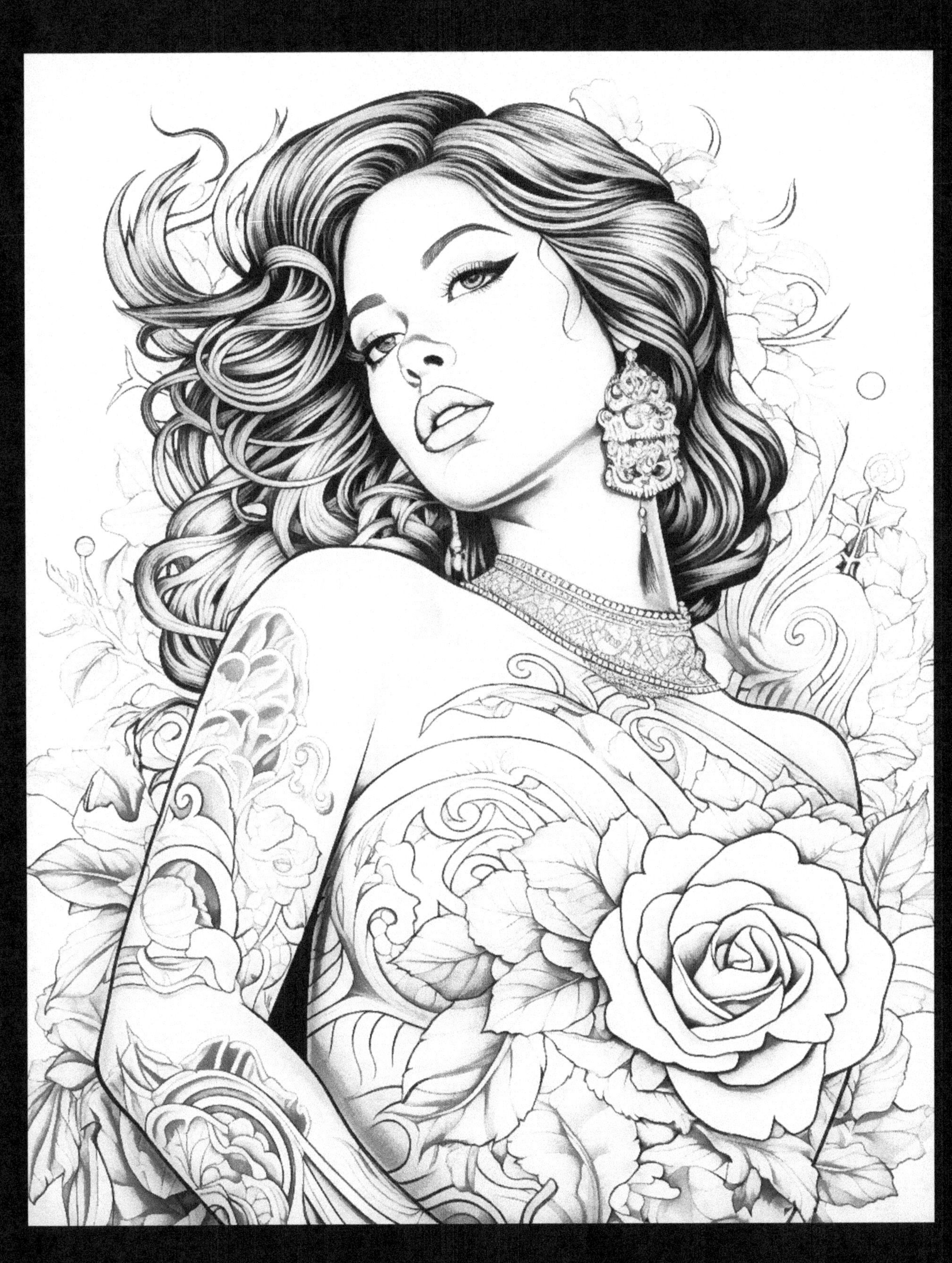

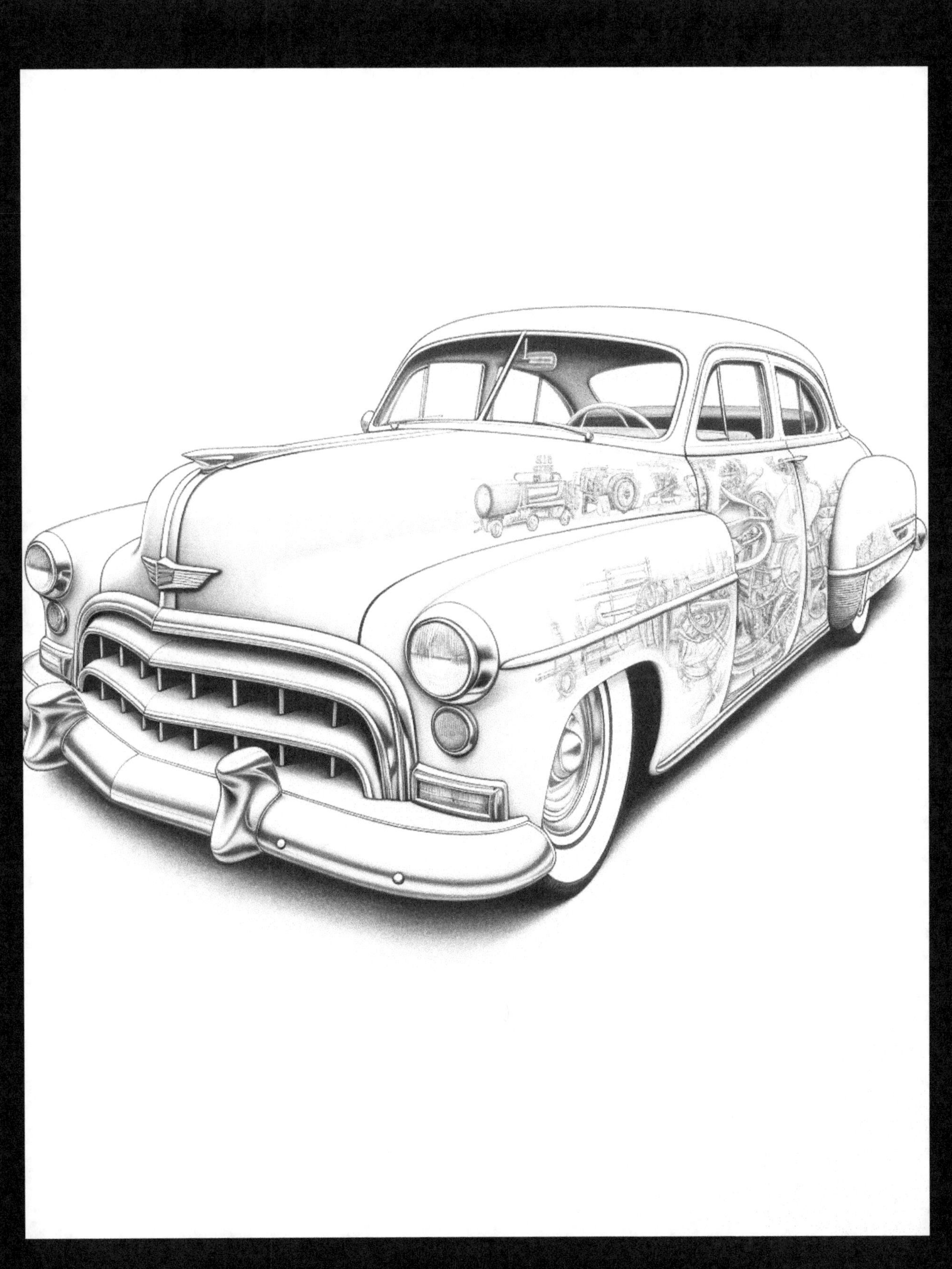

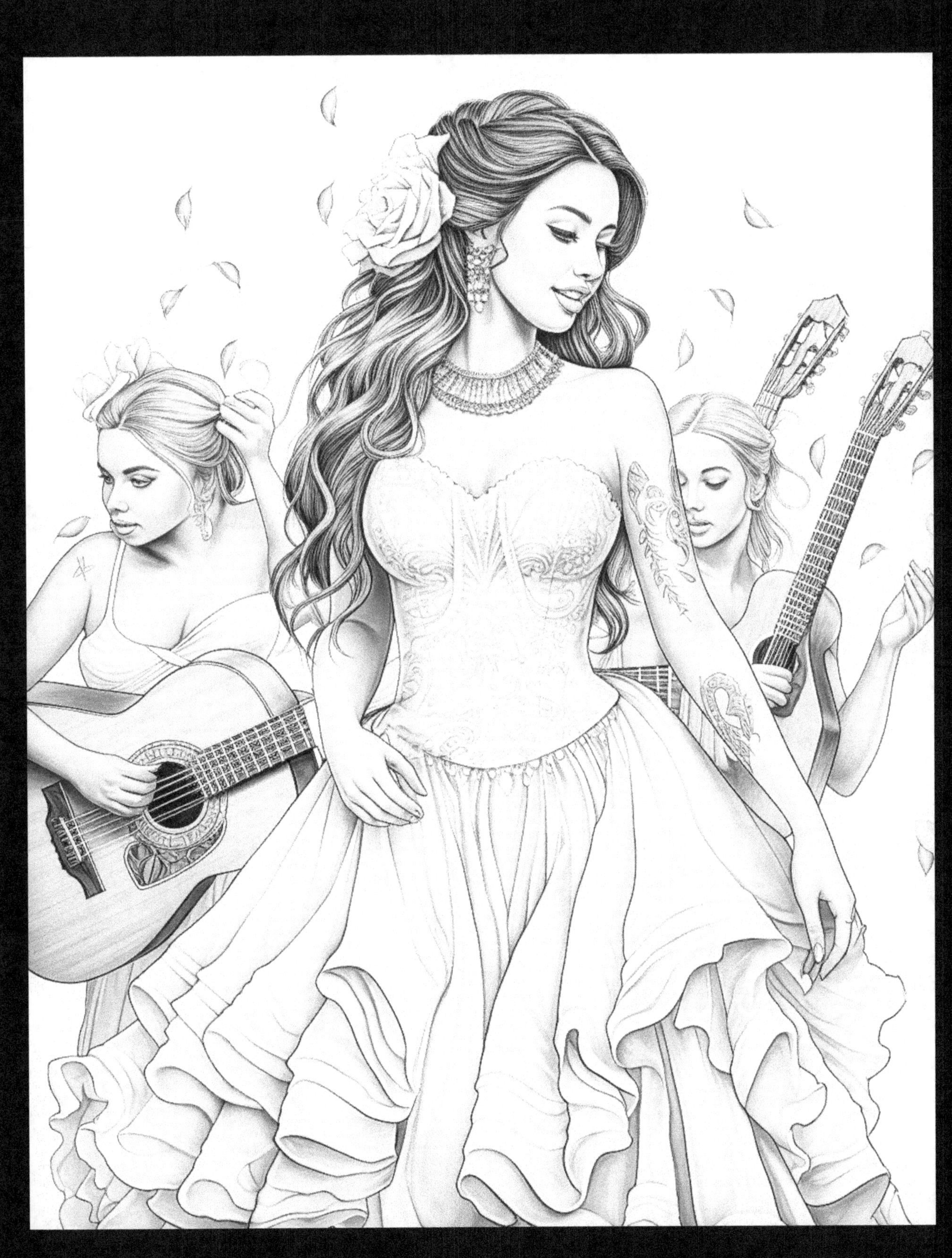

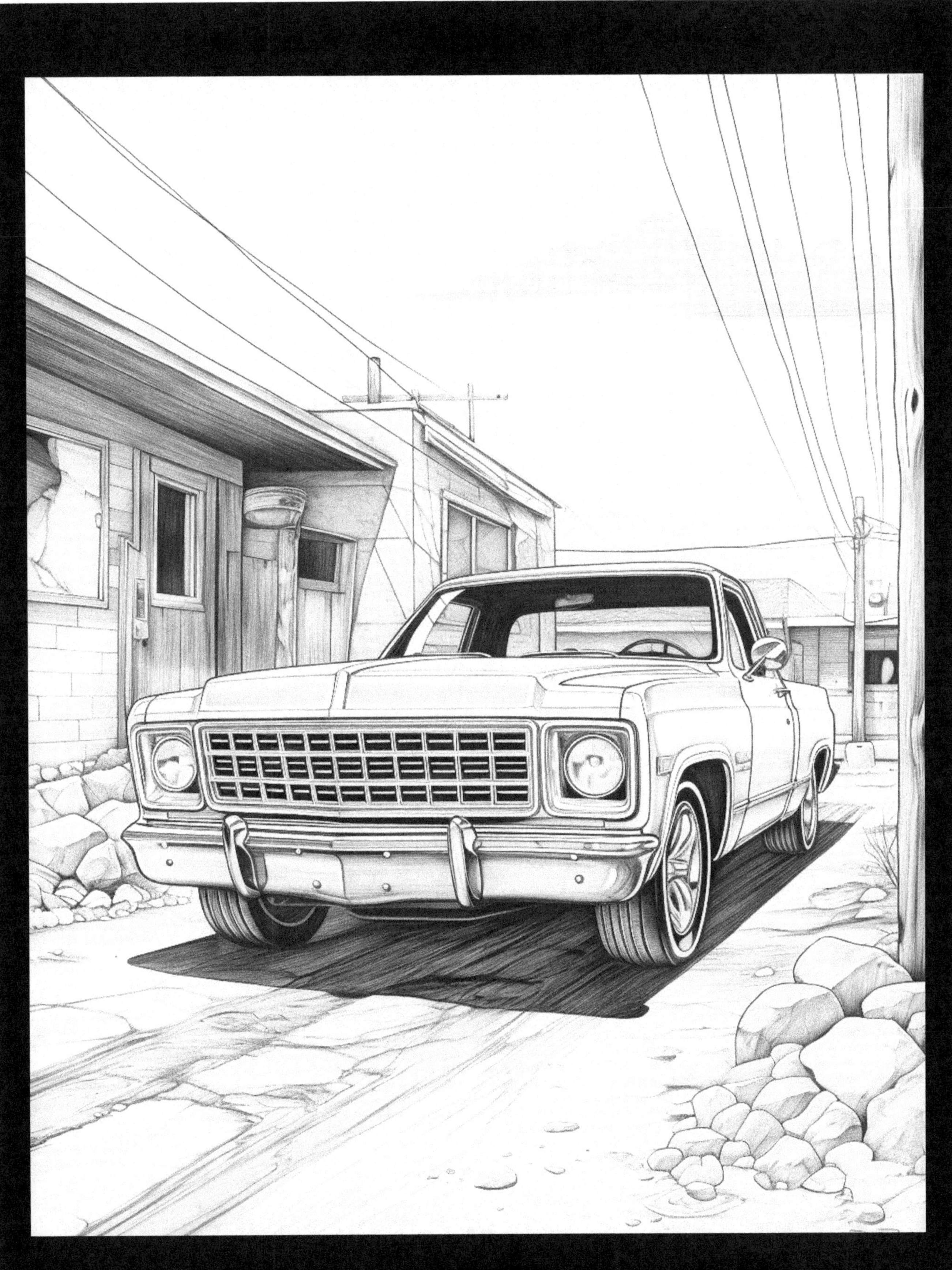

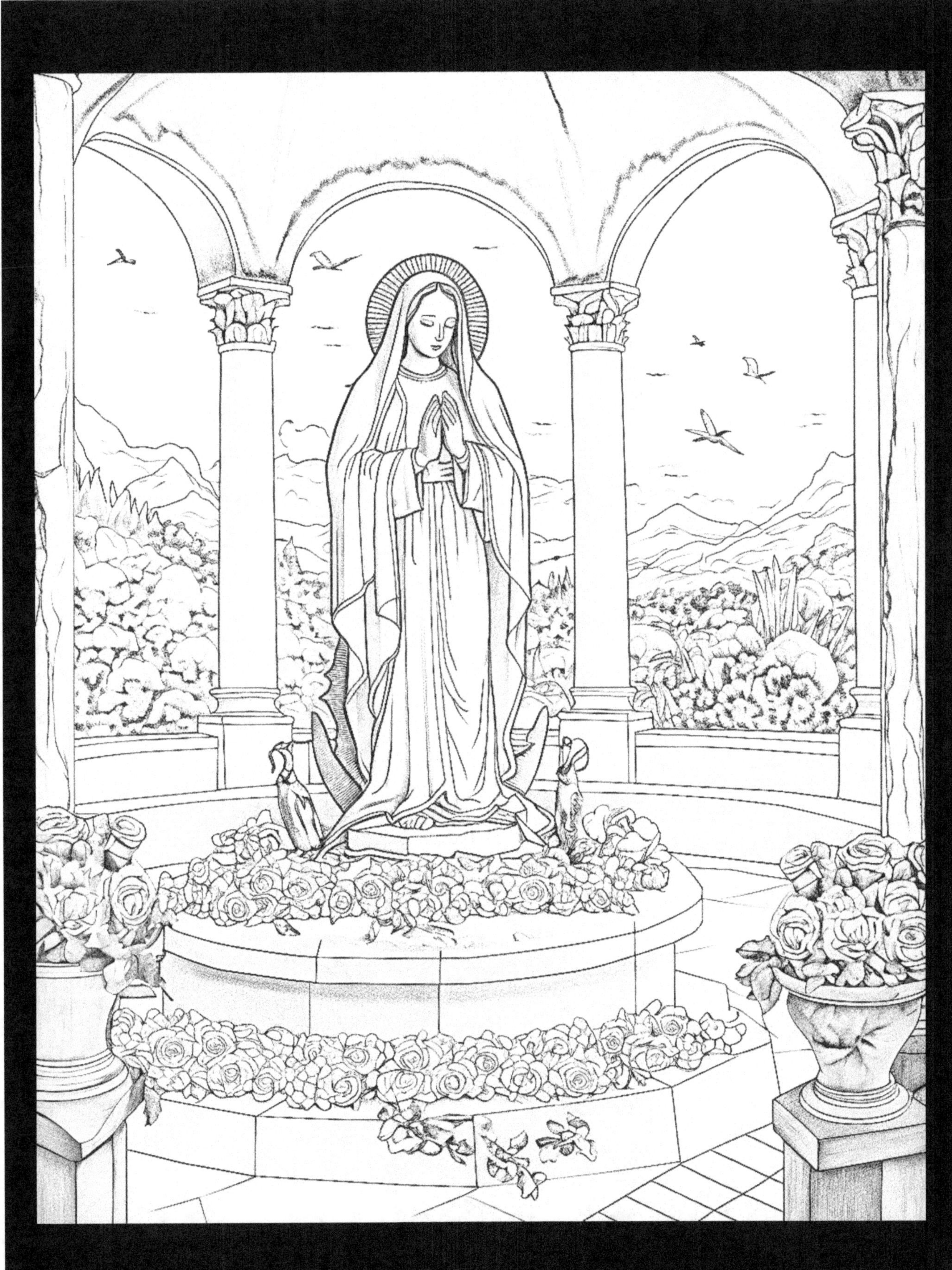

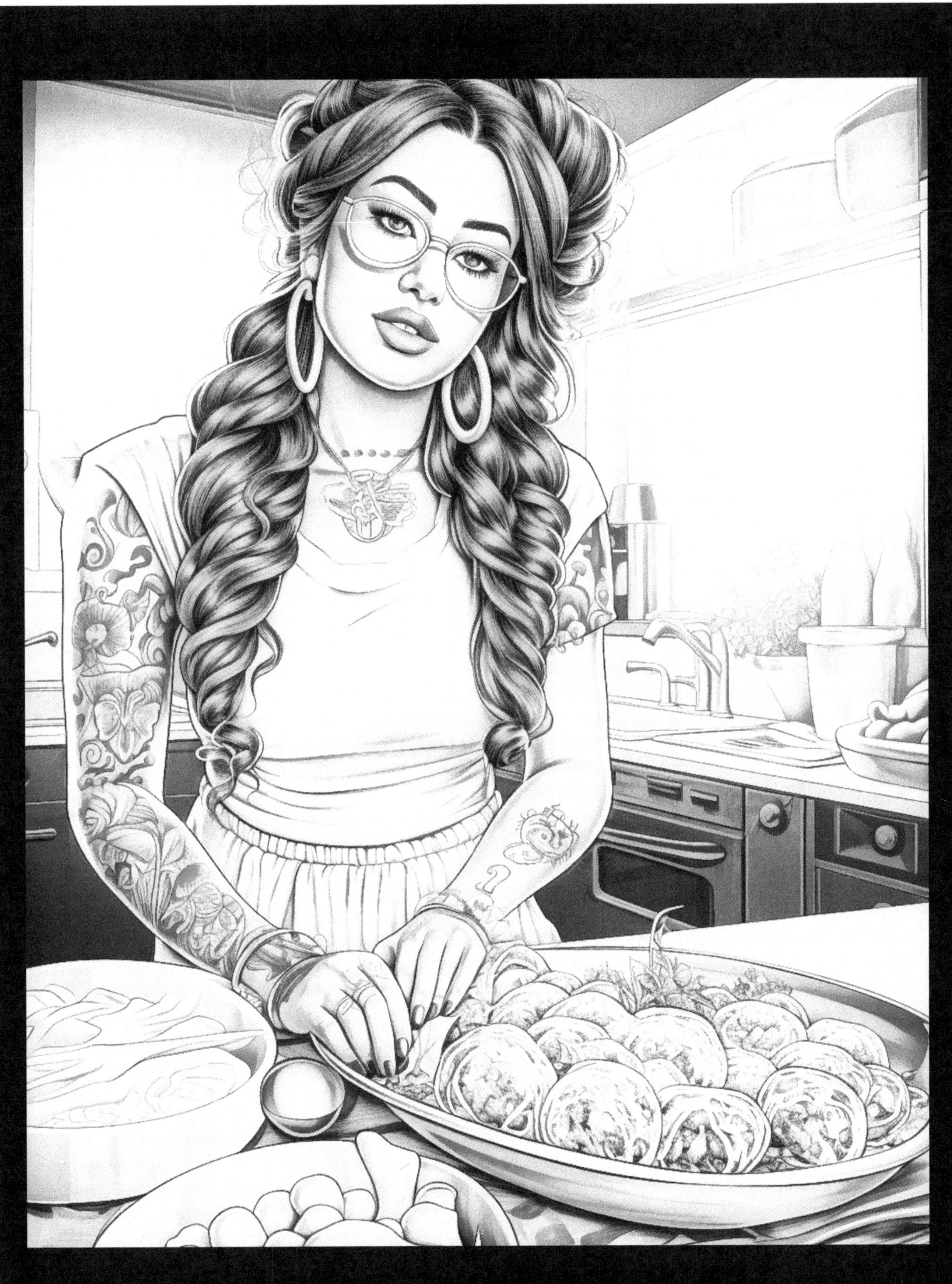

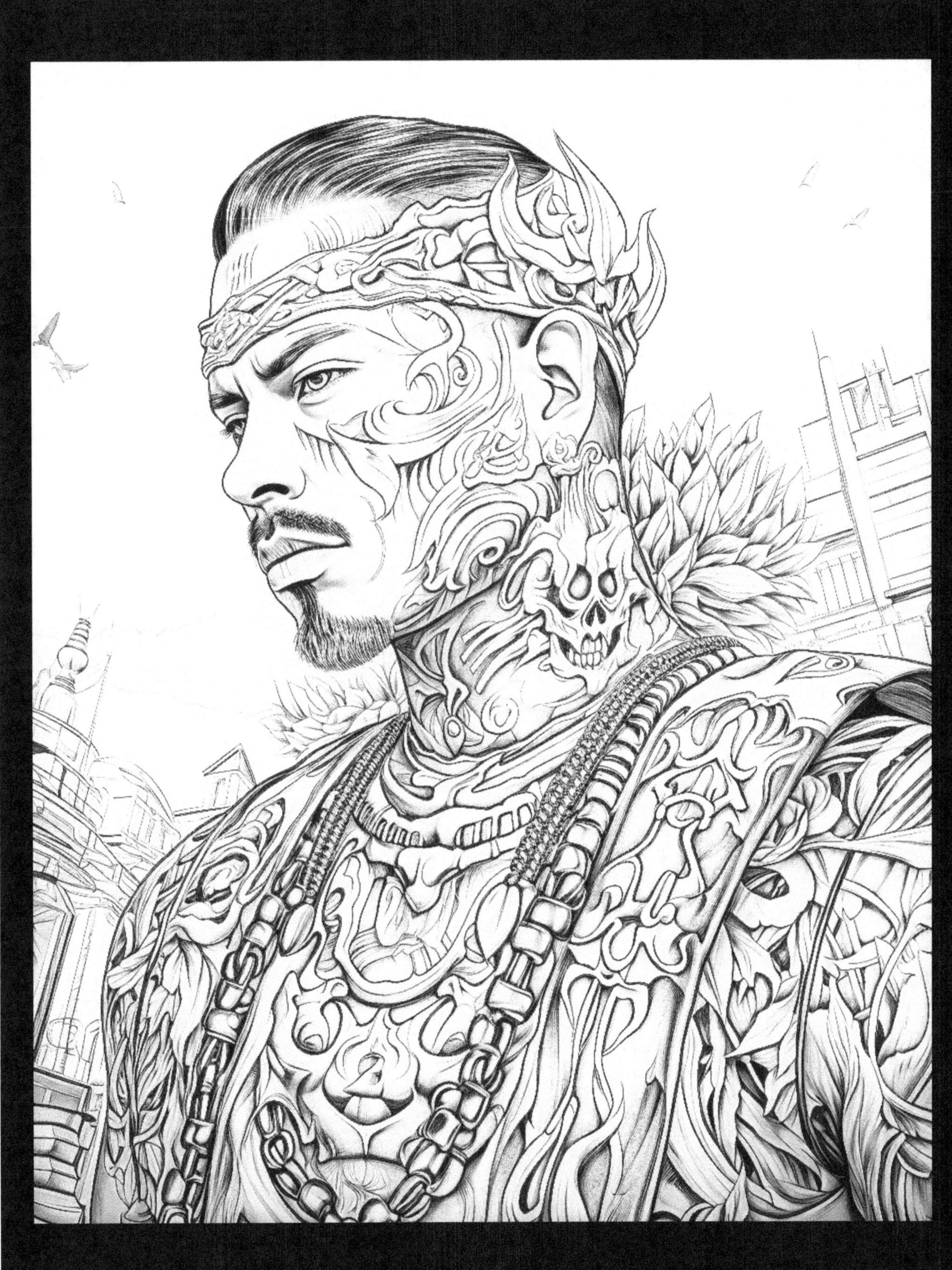

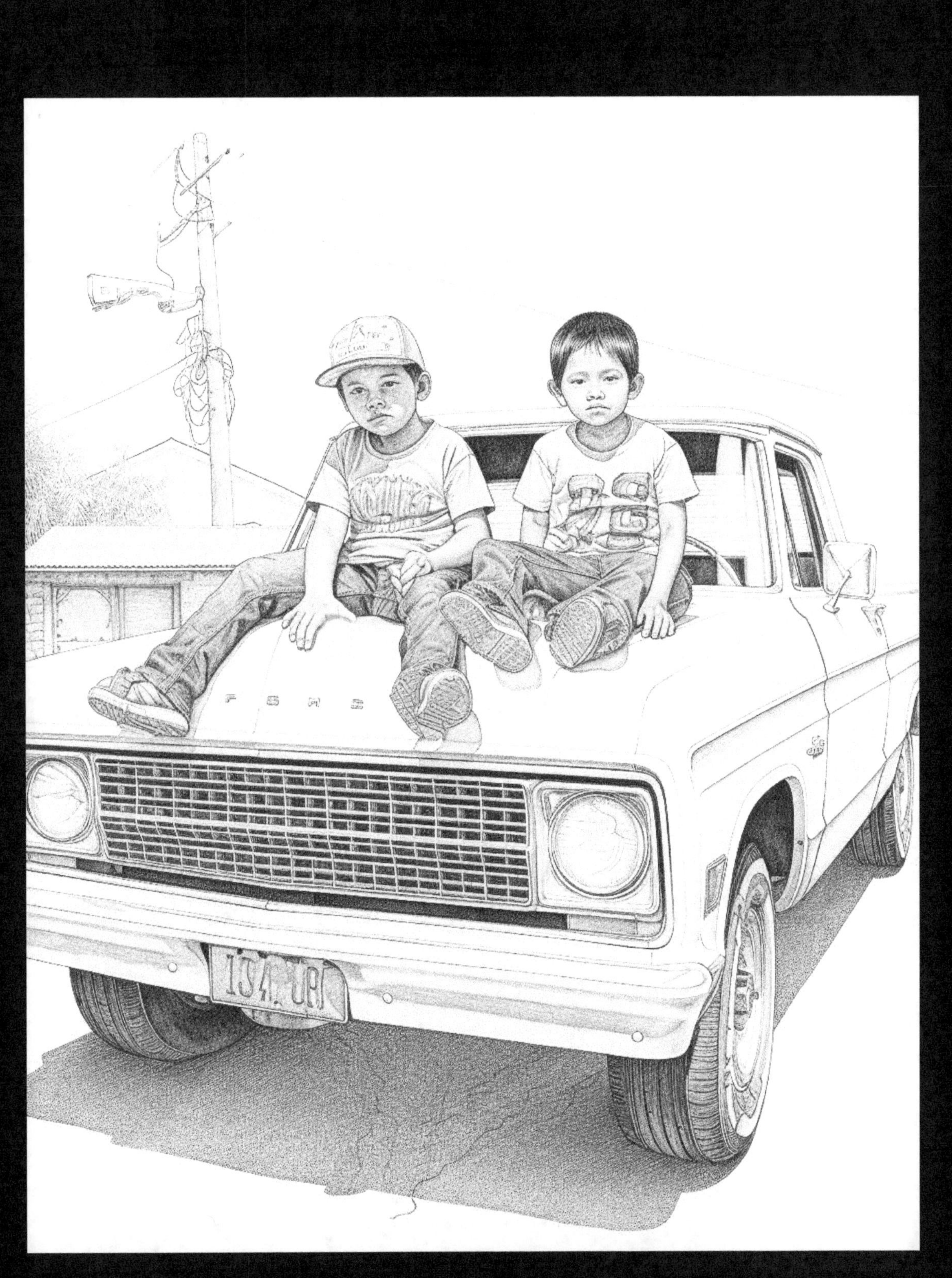
FORD
134 URI

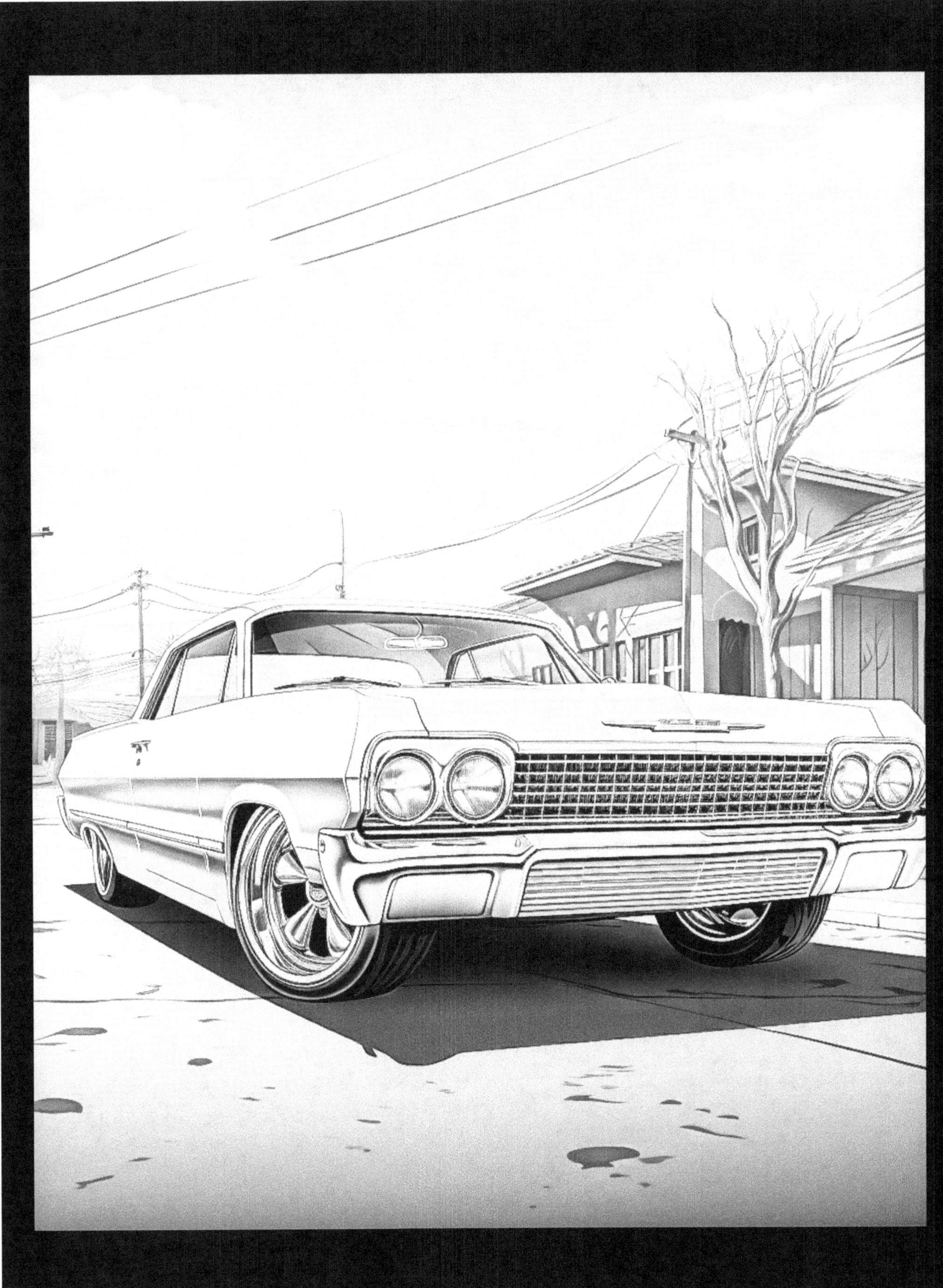

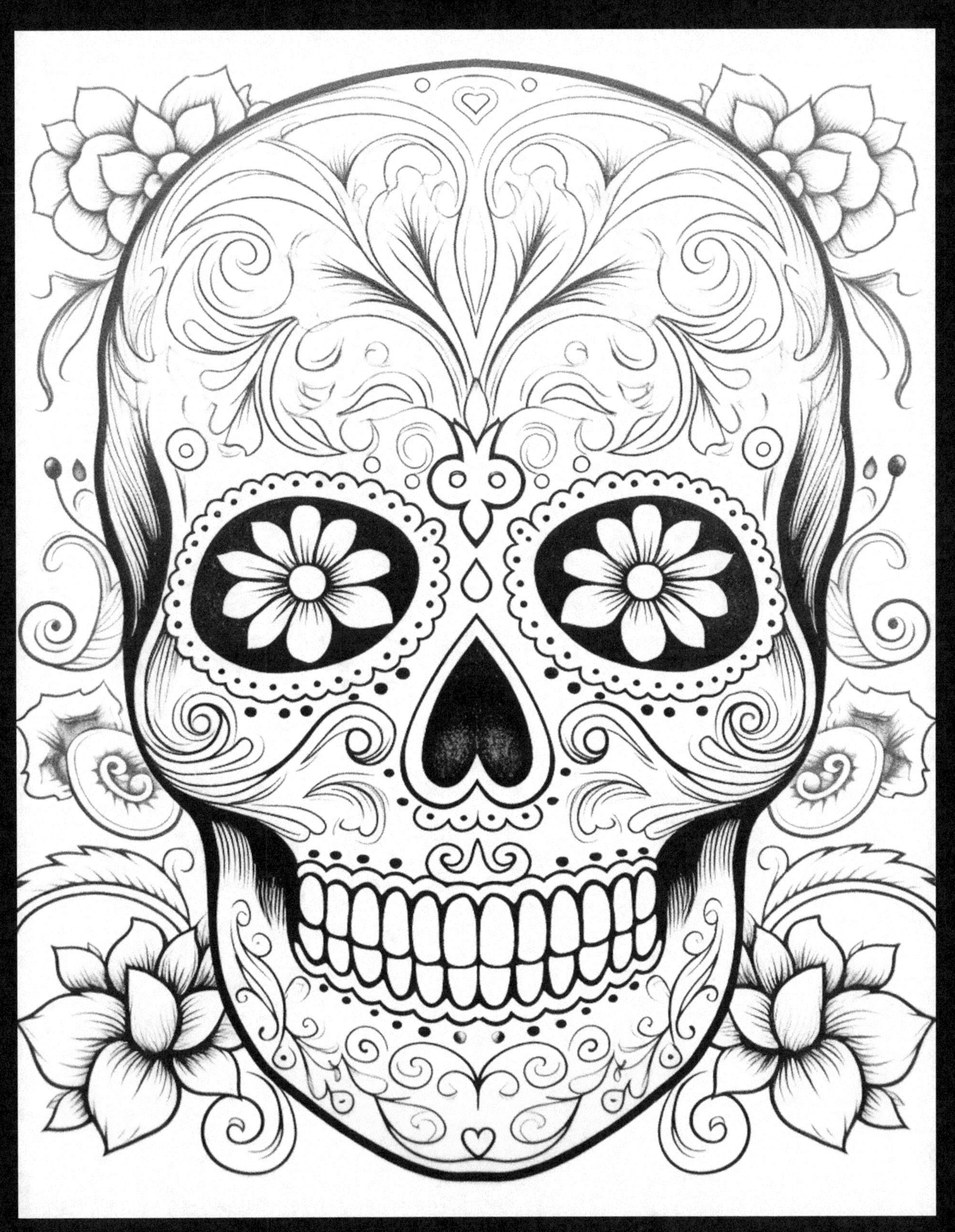

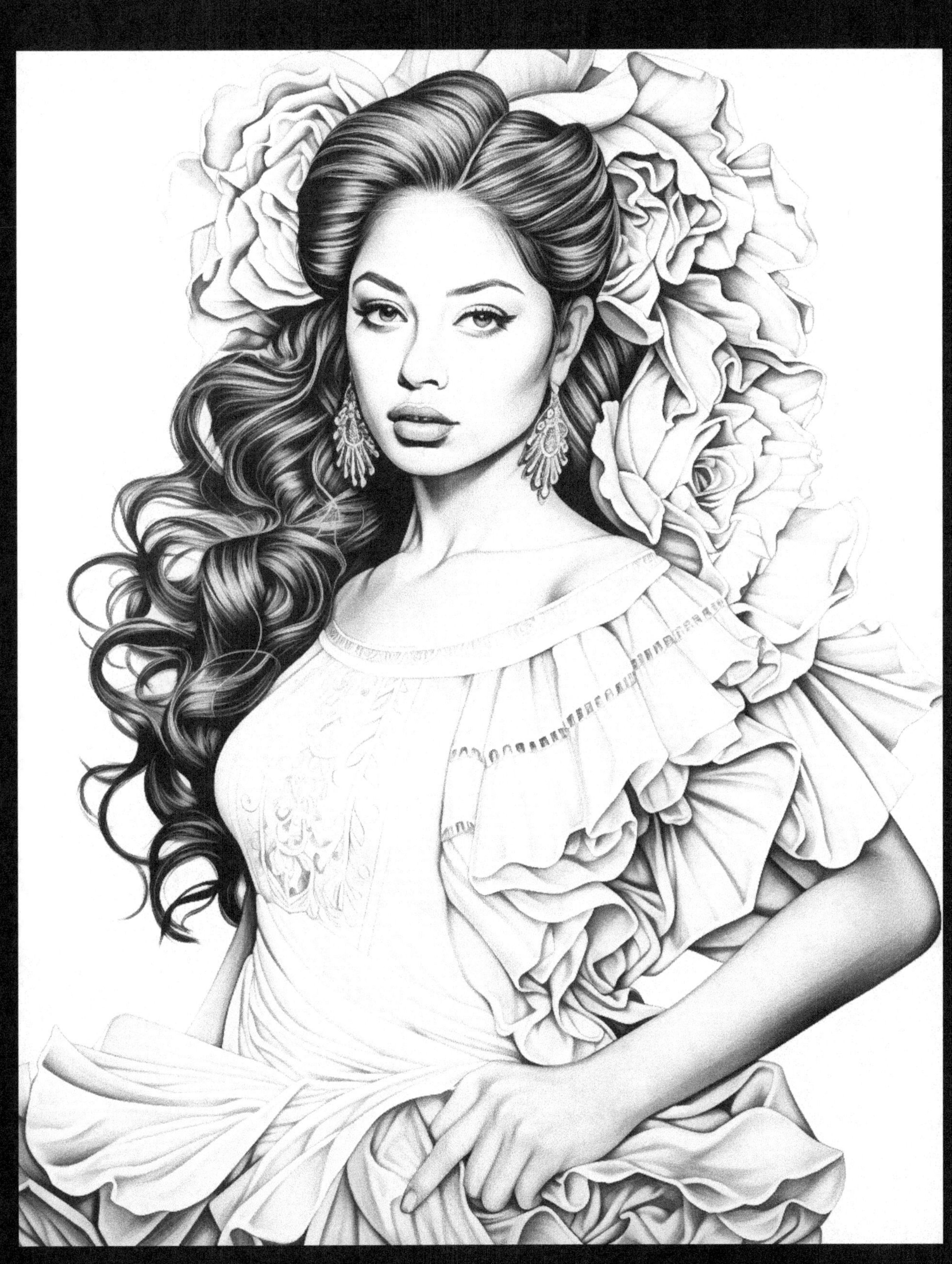

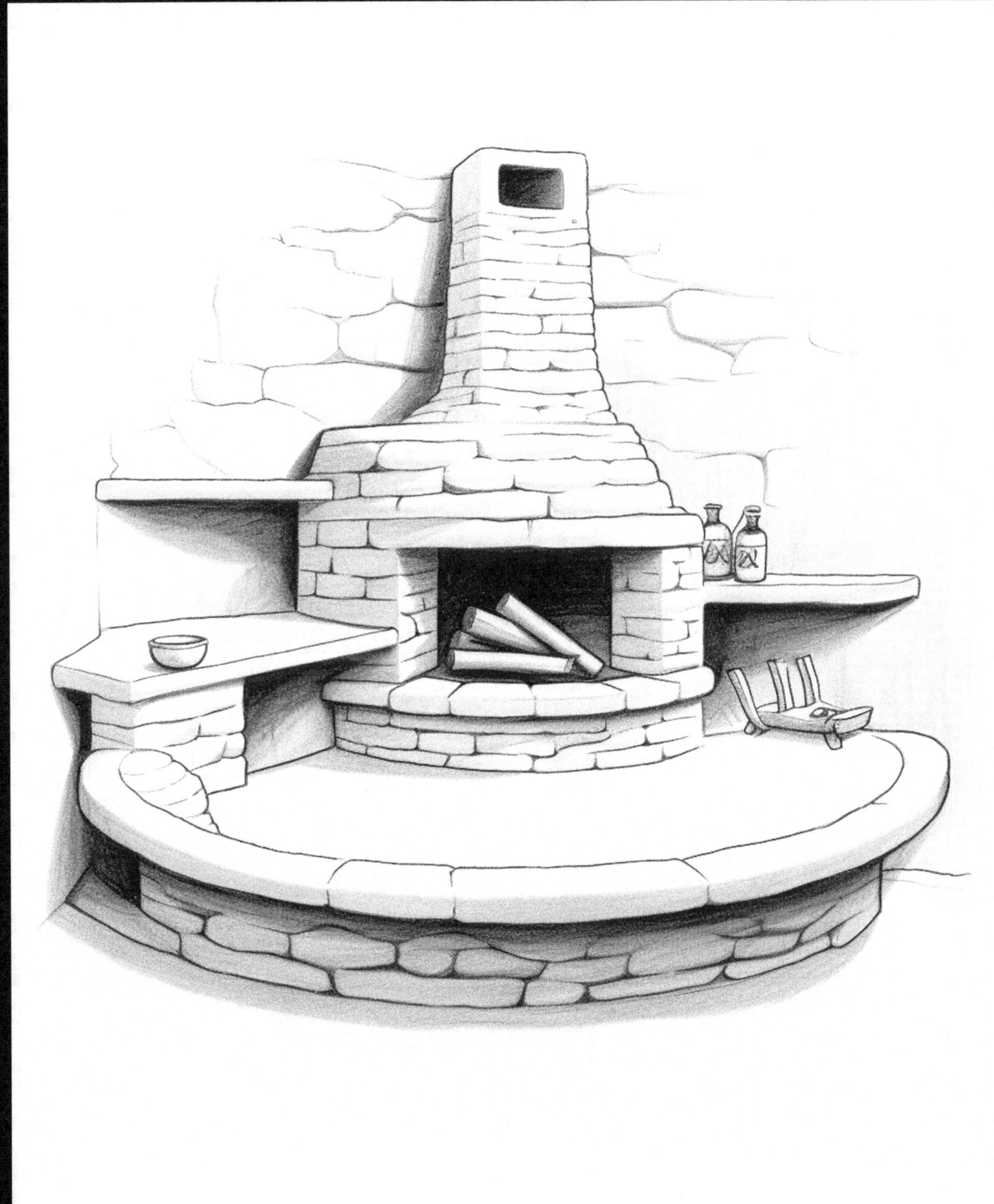

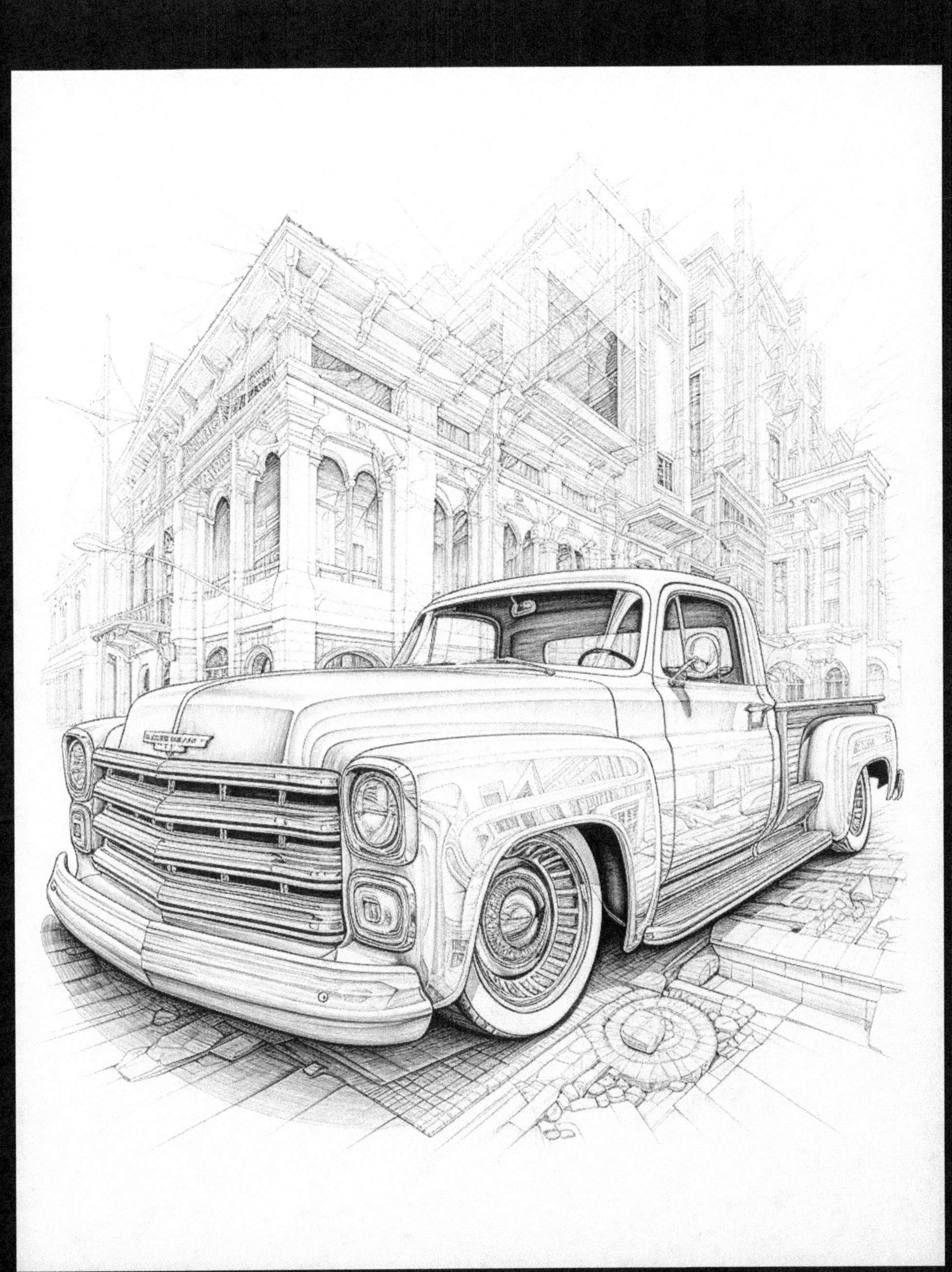

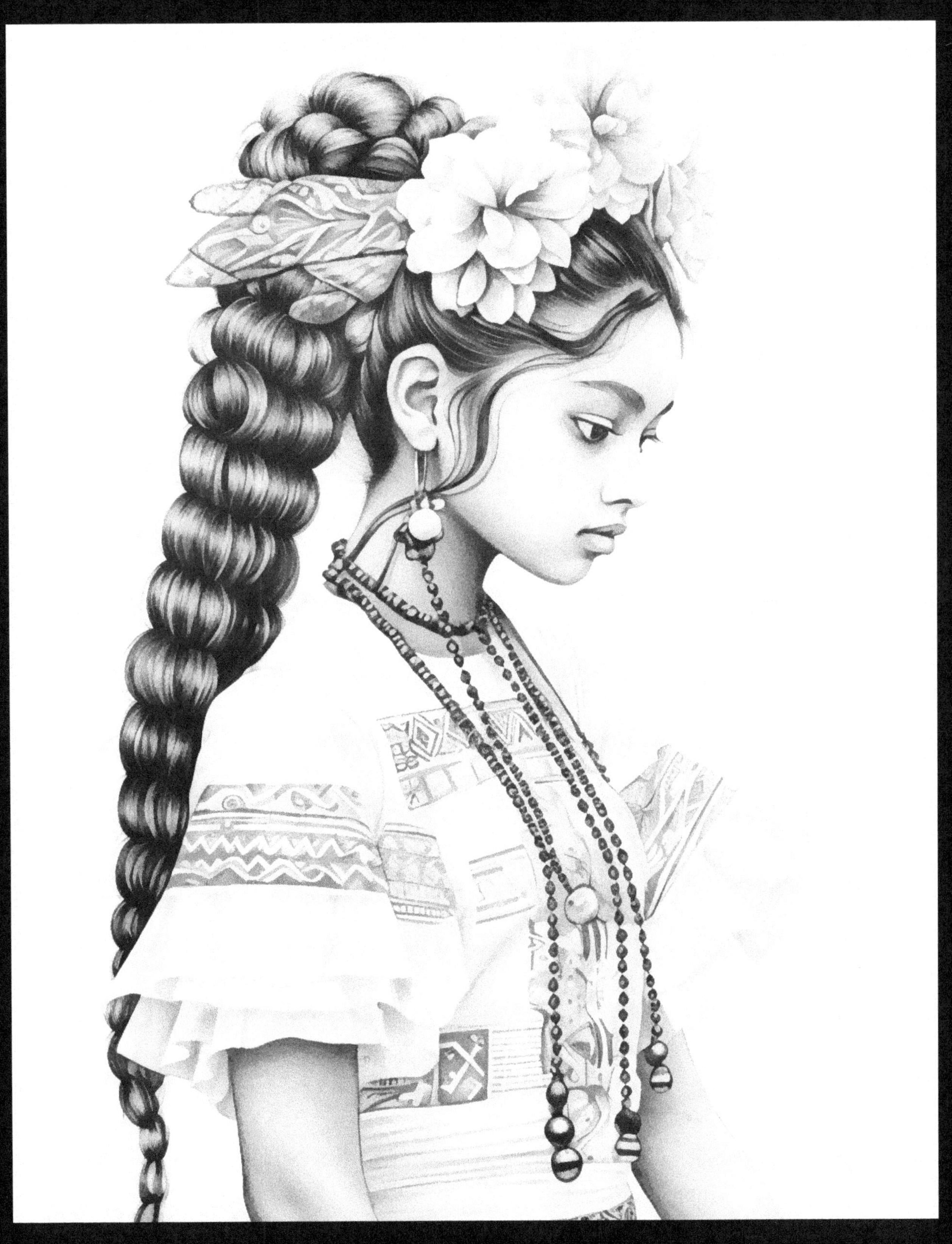

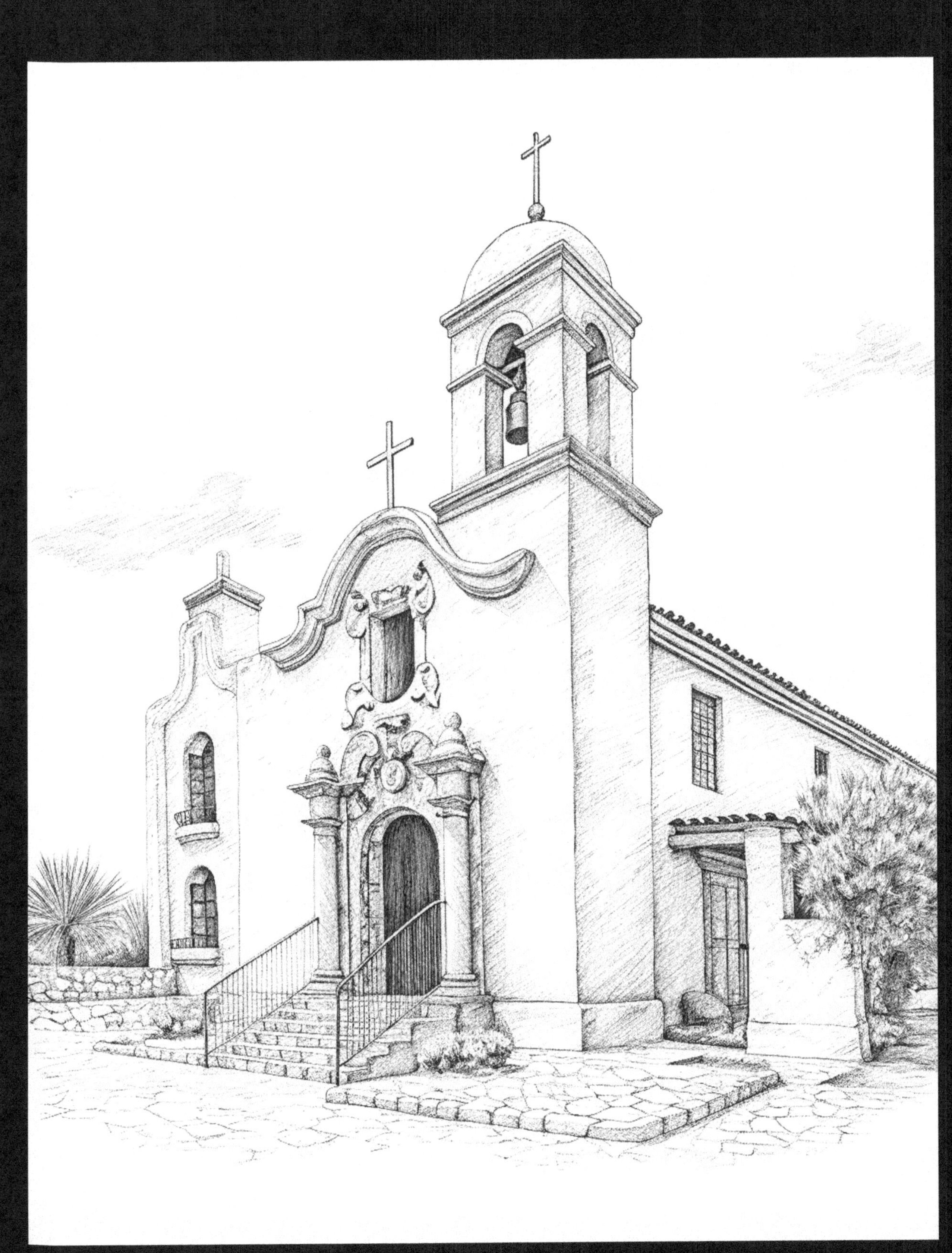

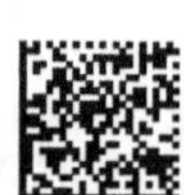

www.ingramcontent.com/pod-product-compliance
Lightning Source LLC
Chambersburg PA
CBHW080027260726
48658CB00007B/2511